Ramblings, Rhymes and East End Times
(Three an~~

I hope that I can
Or even ma
I hope I make you s
And maybe w
But mostly just to entertain
And pass an hour or two
As I write down my take on life
And pass it on to you ...

Also from this author:

The Ramblings of a Would Be East End Poet
(Pie and Mash)

More Ramblings of a Would Be East End poet
(Pie and Mash 2)

Relax a little, take some time
and join me in my life of rhyme

Happy Reading

God Bless

Chris Ross...xx

I'm that Little Boy from Salmen St.

I'm that little boy from down Salmen St
With National Health glasses, sucking a sweet
Socks at half mast and baggy short trousers
Playing on debris and in bombed out houses

I'm the scooter boy with the shiny Lambretta
Sheepskin coat and a tank top sweater
The child of the fifties, the sixties survivor
The bloke down the pub, I'm the mini cab driver

I'm the guy who plays a few chords on guitar
The singer of songs, the would be rock star
Father and Son, Grandad and Brother
Best friend forever, Husband and Lover

I'm the guy in the suit at the business meeting
The West Ham supporter who never stops Tweeting
Serious sometimes but ever the joker
Fan of Sinatra and long time ex smoker

I'm the fella who once had a huge heart attack
The fella the National Health service brought back
Traveller, Home bird and writer of rhymes
Positive always and Grumpy sometimes

I'm the old bloke sitting by a hotel pool
Wearing a tee shirt that says Old Guys Rule
Still wearing glasses and still sucking a sweet
I'm that little boy from down Salmen St

The Kids Have Gone back to School

That's it the kids have gone back to school
Like uniformed lambs to the slaughter
And the young Mums and Dads are feeling quite sad
And missing their Son or their Daughter

The kisses and tears and the hopes and the fears
For those who are now in year one
Left at the school gate as the Mums stand and wait
Wondering what is to come

The morning bell rings and the kids have gone in
Another tear rolls down Mum's cheek
And the cars drive away as if in a parade
They turn around for one last peek

Now year two to six is a different mix
Everyone knows what to expect
The kids want to go and the Mums soon let go
And the tears are now just for effect

The kids of eleven are now in year seven
And were dropped round the corner this time
The hopes and the fears
ain't changed much through the years
But the kids tell their Mums that it's fine

The tears for them now shed in private
Cos at eleven you have to be cool
And life carries on like it always has done
Now the kids have all gone back to school

Angels with Dirty Faces

With the tin bath in front of the fire
And a curtain instead of a door
Angels with dirty faces
Splash water all over the floor

Mum went to get some more water
From the Ascot up over the sink
My brother was farting and we were both laughing
His bath bubbles didn't half stink

We both washed our faces and our other places
And mum washed us behind the ears
We really weren't keen if you know what I mean
And it quite often ended in tears

But then we'd just play in the water
'til mum said enough is enough
"Get him out first", was a line well rehearsed
But then came the bit that we loved

Mum got the towels from in front of the fire
And wrapped us both up one by one
For Angels with dirty faces
Bath night was a whole lot of fun

Baking

Now, as you know, I like a bit of baking
No not Bacon, though I do like that as well
It's just that I've got hooked on this Mary Berry book
And that's the story I'm about to tell

I've made a cake with Apples and Sultanas
I've also made a Lemon Drizzle cake
I've made a cake with Walnuts and Bananas
And a Fruit and Nut one just for old time's sake

Then when the kids were coming for the weekend
I thought I'd rustle up a little treat
So I made a cake with Clementines and Almonds
And trust me that was good enough to eat

Now there's the problem, all you do is eat 'em
I'm always popping out there to the tin
I cut myself a little slice, and then I say ooh that was nice
How does Mary Berry stay so slim ?

Now, I'm not quite ready yet to go on Bake Off
I don't think that my cakes are that highbrow
I think I'll make a Chocolate cake with Baileys this weekend
And I might just have a Bacon Sandwich now

Breakfast in Bed

I dropped Mary off at the station this morning
And came home and got back into bed
I was snug as a bug in a soft quilted rug
And I loved it, it has to be said

I know that it's Monday morning
But there's nothing that I need to do
So I've just now got up, made a steaming hot cup
And I'm sat here now talking to you

I don't have a plan for the rest of the day
How much better than this does it get
But I thought that I'd better say Good Morning world
In case later on I forget

Now as I look out my window
I see it's beginning to snow
In case you haven't looked out of your window
I thought that you might like to know

I've just heard the pop of the toaster
And the marmalade waits to be spread
I've felt the tea pot and it's still nice and hot
I'll see you later ... Breakfast in Bed

Checking In

The bloke next to me stinks of garlic
Lord knows what he ate last night
And the woman behind, can't seem to find
Her ticket to get on this flight

There's a couple with two rowdy children
I'll bet that they're sat next to me
Mary's nowhere in sight as they've opened our flight
As usual she's gone for a wee

There's a girl with an overstuffed suitcase
Who's arguing with the ground staff
It can't be too heavy, I weighed it already
I think that she's having a laugh

I can see Mary coming towards me
And she don't seem to be in a hurry
I'm only two people away from the front
And as ever beginning to worry

There's a little girl in her pyjamas
And a baldy bloke drinking a beer
A young courting couple who could soon be in trouble
All human life is right here

Then we finally arrive at the front of the queue
And at last we get rid of our cases
Old garlic breath's gone and the kids have moved on
Aren't airports wonderful places ? ...

Cutting the Grass

We've just been out to cut the grass
Well, I use the Royal We
One of us laid in the deckchair, sunbathing
And the other one was Me

Strimmer round the edges
Mower on the lawn
Oops! .. I think I've woke her up
No it was only a yawn

But that's it done and dusted
But the garden now looks bigger
But how could that be, Oh don't ask me
Next time I'll need a big digger

I must admit I'm a bit sleepy
But some jobs need to be done
And thanks to Mary at least I don't...
...have to lay out and sleep in the sun

So back to work tomorrow
I'm really excited about that
I couldn't be happier if I was twins
With a Russian Girl wearing a hat

I've no idea what that means
But be honest, at least it's a rhyme
I think I'll shut my eyes for an hour
Let's face it, It's probably time

A New Pair of Jeans

I wanted to get a new pair of jeans
But jeans ain't that easy to choose
With so many different styles and designs
It's easy to get, well confused

Now there's dark ones and light ones,
loose ones and tight ones
High waist or under the belly
Comfort or Boot fit, laid back or loose fit
Or the ones that I saw on the telly ?

Well of course there's your Levi 501s
But I don't know what 501 means
Do they do any other combination of numbers?
I just want a new pair of jeans

And then of course there's your designers
But the choices ain't always that clear
Diesel, Armani, Jeff banks or Versace
And besides which, they're too flippin' dear

Now I've looked in the Gap and in Debenhams
And the Ben Sherman shop in Lakeside
I even tried Top Man and Primark
With Mary along for the ride

...

I've been into Next but came out of there vexed
And I'm sure that you won't disagree
That when I see "Skinny" on labels on clothes
I know they ain't talking to me

So zip fly or buttons, cut outs or cut ins
And whether in Black, Greys or Blues
I just wanted to get a new pair of jeans
But jeans ain't that easy to choose

You Can't even Tell it was There

A block of flats straddles the street I grew up in
You can't even tell it was there
The windows and doors,
that were ours and next doors
All gone as if nobody cared

The pub on the corner demolished
The houses we lived in pulled down
The factories and shops
and at least two bus stops
And I don't recognise my own town

The docks and the bombed out houses
And the debris where we used to play
The goal that we painted up there on the wall
And the cobbled stones .. all swept away

And all in the name of progress
Cos they said our old houses were slums
Well a two up two down on the east side of town
Would today fetch a nice tidy sum

I know that the flats were more modern
With bathrooms and bedrooms to spare
But a block of flats straddles the street I grew up in
You can't even tell it was there

Re-tweet

I re-tweeted something that somebody tweeted,
'cos I thought that was how Twitter rolled
They tweet it, you tweet it, someone else re-tweets it
On and on 'til it gets old

The account was a bookshop in Paris
I certainly meant no offence
But in some kind of rage, they've blocked me from their page
It just doesn't make any sense

They tweeted a tweet about poetry
A light hearted line someone said
I just made a joke about buying my book
And re-tweeted and then went to bed

D'you think it's connected with Brexit
Waterloo, or perhaps Agincourt
Or they just weren't keen, for their tweet to be seen
But I thought that's what Twitter is for

But I'm not going to take it too personally
I'm just gonna let this one pass
But I'll tell you what, bookshop in Paris
Take your twitter feed and tenir votre ane ...

Bonjour ...xx

Layers

Now as you know, I like a cup of coffee
But you just can't beat a lovely cup of tea
I also like a Pasta Carbonara
But Pie and Mash will always win for me

I like to go on holiday quite often
But coming home is always in the plan
I like to watch Real Madrid play football
But you know I'll always be a West Ham fan

I like a glass of fine red wine with dinner
But sometimes you just can't beat a can of beer
I'm big and brave and hard while watching Rocky
But Bambi always makes me shed a tear

I never watch X Factor on the telly
But believe that Cheryl is a national treasure
I'm a fan of Willie Nelson and Sinatra
But the Spice Girls are my secret guilty pleasure

You see, I've got as many layers as an onion
And so have you and everybody else
Is anyone the person that you always thought they were?
And are you always honest with yourself

There's a Screaming Competition up in Lakeside

There's a screaming competition up in Lakeside
Just for kids up to the age of three
The heats are being held in all the restaurants
But I'm not sure where the final's gonna be

The early stages seem to be in Costa
There's a kid in there who's face is turning blue
His mum's just put his picture up on snapchat
And his dad looks like he hasn't got a clue

There's a couple kicking off now in the Wimpy
Though one of them, I think is over age
I know he'll be disqualified, but then again at least he tried
And found a way to let go of his rage

The quarter final seems to be in Strada
There's three of them in there to say the least
So we go into Nando's, 'cos it seems that's where the Nans go
Just to hide and try to get some peace

But someone sneaks one in while we're not looking
And this one makes the final, that's for sure
With lungs like Pavarotti as they take away her bottie
And her mum and Dad both smile like that's a cure

Well anyway it's time for us to leave now
But if you've got nowhere you'd rather be
There's a screaming competition up in Lakeside
But I'd have to say I'd rather you than me

A Ride on the District Line

Today I went on the District Line
From Plaistow to Stepney Green
It's been a good while and I did have to smile
At some of the places I've seen

West Ham station and Bromley by Bow
Bow Road then on to Mile End
Stations I used all the time as a nipper
Stations I ain't seen since then

The thing that struck me as I sat there
Was that nothing much seems to have changed
The benches and fences and ticket hall entrance
All seem to look just the same

It's like going back on a trip through my youth
And it left me a bit Dewey eyed
I can't help but laugh about times that have passed
And the stops that we made on that ride

Like Upton Park Station on a Saturday
Where the Hammers would hopefully win
Or the Moonie by Stepney Green Station
Where we all used to go for a swim

...

...

Or the hospital up in Whitechapel
For our eye tests and dentist and stuff
And we lived in Mile End so our journey would end
In the place that we knew and we loved

I'm glad that I went on the District Line
And I'm glad that it's not changed that much
It's like one of those virtual reality rides
Only this one you can reach out and touch

When you Wake up in the Morning

When you wake up in the morning in the sunshine
And you haven't got too many aches and pains
When your first thought is
"I wonder what this sunny day will bring"
And not "I want to go to sleep again"

When the shower seems inviting and refreshing
And your curtains rustle in the summer breeze
When your coffee smells like heaven
and your clock says ten past seven
And the birds are singing outside in the trees

When you sit and eat your breakfast in the garden
And the smell of summer flowers fills the air
When you start and read a page or two
from a book that someone gave to you
And realise you still have time to spare

When you pour yourself a second cup of coffee
And watch a squirrel dance along the wall
When the sun begins to warm your skin
to match the glow you have within
You know that life ain't too bad after all ...

Say Hello

If you're sitting drinking coffee round in Costa
And you see someone who looks a bit like me
And he's slowly drinking skinny latte from a paper cup
And you look across and wonder could that be

If you're loading up your trolley over Asda
And you hear a voice you think you recognise
If he's laughing with the girls there on the checkout
In honesty, you shouldn't be surprised

If you're on a bus and heading for the city
And you see someone you think you kind of know
If you think you've seen that face before but then again
you're not too sure
Why not take a chance and say hello

It's probably me and I swear I'm fully house-trained
On top of that I promise I won't bite
Unless of course you've got a bar of Cadbury's Fruit and Nut
And then just mind your fingers 'cos I might

When London is in her Pyjamas

When London is in her Pyjamas
And most of us tucked up in bed
The lights are turned off in the theatres
And the traffic lights flash green to red

When the city's bereft of it's workers
And it's alleys and passageways dark
The dustcarts have cleaned up the rubbish
And they've padlocked the gates at the park

It's then that the ghosts of old London
Awaken and wander again
From the streets outside old Newgate prison
Through to Ave Maria Lane

From the site where the Smithfield gallows once stood
Where it's said that Braveheart met his end
To the Tower of London and through Traitors Gate
The spectres will wander again

Down Whitechapel way where the Ripper held sway
To the plague pits of Liverpool Street
Dead and undead, Ghouls and Ghosts
You never know who you might meet

I Don't Know

There's lots of stuff that we all know
And then there's stuff that just we know
And also stuff that they all know
That no one ever told us

And then there's stuff we think we know
And stuff that we make out we know
And also stuff we'll never know
'cos they aren't gonna tell us

There's stuff that we don't need to know
And stuff that we don't want to know
And it's a good job though that we don't know
'cos it would just confuse us

So, if there's something that you know
And you think that we all should know
Tell us now, you never know
It may even amuse us

But what I know is what I know
And by this time, I'm sure you know
That I don't know and that's all I know
And from there on Heaven help us

I Can Still taste the Fish Paste Sandwiches

I can still taste the fish paste sandwiches
And the tea that was poured from a flask
As we spent the whole day on the beach at Thorpe Bay
And watched as the tankers sailed past

I remember the chocolate Club biscuits
That mum always took for a treat
Unwrapping and slipping them back in their sleeve
Making them easy to eat

The beach huts that ran down the seafront
And the cockle shells spread all around
The buckets and spades and castles we made
And collecting the stones that we'd found

I can still feel those hard plastic sandals
That we wore when we went in the sea
I can still hear the sqwalk of the seagulls
As they circled and terrorised me

I remember the Calamine lotion
Mum pasted on when we got burnt
She'd say everyday it would all end this way
But back then we just never learnt
...

...

I can still feel the sand in my underpants
As we changed to go home on the beach
And my nan held a towel up around us
And gave us a mint humbug each

I can hear the doors slam on the train going home
As the guard whistled us on our way
I can still taste the fish paste sandwiches
If I drive down the front at Thorpe Bay

No E or U

Now, since the Brits voted for Brexit
Well, Brussels have thrown a big strop
There's a couple of things that annoy them
And they're telling us we have to stop

We can't use the letters EU any more
We just have to pass them both by
So some of our spelling, will need some re-telling
So why don't we give it a try

Now some words we'll lose altogether
Because they won't make any sense
Like Cucumber, Queue and Underwear
Ounces and Pounces and Pence

Eerie and Query and Equerry
Would all just be too hard to change
Sleeplessness would be unpronounceable
And Unpronounceable will too need to change

In some places we'll use a W
Like Qwickly and Qwietly and Qwaint
As ever though Queer could be tricky
But Qwality certainly ain't

So Europe will just be called Rop now
Or we could say Enough is Enough
We could loop the L and the I together
And tell Brussels that they can Flick off

Old Bloke M.O.T.

I'm gonna see the quack again tomorrow
I'm going for an old bloke M.O.T
I thought that it was time I saw the Doctor
And he thought it was time that he saw me

I've got a couple things that need discussing
But I'll leave them for tomorrow for your sake
I'm sure that you don't want to know about
my breathing and my flow
And how my right foot always seems to ache

I'm sure he'll take some blood and whassname samples
I know he'll tell me that I'm overweight
But I hope he doesn't mention, cholesterol or hypertension
'cos that's more tablets that I'll have to take

I'm going on a diet once I've seen him
I'll join a gym and maybe even jog
I'll get myself a bike and go out riding when I like
And I'll end up fitter than a butcher's dog

But for now I have to go to see the Doctor
And ask him why I'm tired all the time
But perhaps he'll tell me all is well,
with my heart and blood and weight as well
And the only problem's that I'm past my prime

3.23 In the Morning

It's pitch dark at 3.23 in the morning,
I'm sure you won't be surprised
But that's the time that I keep waking up,
The time that I open my eyes

Could there be magical forces afoot ?
Could the spirit world come into play?
It's more likely some inconsiderate git,
Beginning or ending their day

Now I like the mornings and watching the Sunrise
Is my favourite time of the day
But 3.23? are you joking with me?
There has to be some other way

I need to investigate what's going on because
Why, is what I need to know
I need the the services of Jessica Fletcher,
Or even that Hercule Poirot

Maybe I'll do the research myself
I'm sure that would be much more fun
I could speak in a fake Belgian accent
And discover the warm smoking gun

Or look startled at being a middle aged woman
Who just wrote a best selling book
Who finds all the clues, puts them together
And invites the policeman to look

...

...

Or maybe Lieutenant Columbo would say,
"I'm sorry, there's just one more thing"
Or Kojak would say "Who loves ya Baby"
But please, never ask him to sing

No I have a better idea than all that,
I know now what I'm going to do
They will not wake me, at 3.23,
I'll set my clock for 3.22....

That'll show 'em ...

I Thought that I Might

I thought that I might cut the grass today
I thought I might go to the shops
I thought that I might clean the car today
But thoughts of all that have to stop

I woke up and found it was raining
And all of my plans went awry
So now today's plan, and just 'cos I can
Is to stay in and keep warm and dry

Or I could grab my coat and umbrella
And go for a walk around town
Splashing in puddles and walking through tunnels
And watching the rain falling down

I could go 'round to Costa for coffee
Without cake, I don't want to be rash
And after my coffee, just like a real Cockney
Could go out and have Pie and Mash

I could jump in the car and go driving
And maybe end up at Southend
Or go to Lakeside, well at least that's inside
But think of the money I'd spend

I'll just drink my tea while I ponder
And the truth is that I'm not complaining
But I thought that I might cut the grass today
And I woke up and found it was raining

The Tea Bag

It's time that we paid tribute to a thing that we hold dear
It's small and white and clean and bright
and round, or even square
It's powers are well known to us and when our spirits flag
We reach for our old friend indeed,
The magical Tea Bag

The drink that cheers and lifts us, the friend that gets us up
It's amazing what that bag can do, with water, in your cup
Now I know some like their coffee, I like a latte too
But no amount of beans can do what that small bag can do

We know about the miracle, of turning water into wine
I don't deny it happened but I weren't there at the time
But every day around our way, it's there for all to see
The miracle of the paper bag,
That turns water into tea

There's no need for a strainer you just throw the bag away
No leaves left in the bottom like there was back in the day
So sweet and milky, smooth and silky or thick and black like tar
Whatever is you favourite way,
The Tea Bag is the star

Poppies are Red

Poppies are Red because Poppies are Red
They don't glorify war, they remember the dead
The Red flower's worn as a constant reminder
Of the Poppies that grew on the graves out in Flanders

Not racist, or divisive but certain and bold
Remembering those who would never grow old
No triumphal slogans, no banners no tags
The humble Red Poppy is nobody's flag

Wear one, don't wear one the choice is for you
But don't try to change it to White, Green or Blue
Remember their lives and the blood that they shed
Poppies are Red because Poppies are Red

Monopoly

By the time you get to my age
You'd have made a few mistakes
You'll have been around the block a bit
And had some lucky breaks
Times when things just didn't go
The way you might have planned
And come across some things in life
You didn't understand

The chances are you've been trouble
But not wound up in jail
You've run out of money and that wasn't funny
But you're here to tell us the tale
You've had your frustrations at some of life's stations
But kept on playing the game
Taken your part and right from the start
Knew everyone's lot was the same

You see, life's like a game of Monopoly
And most of what happens is chance
We roll the dice, we don't think twice
And when we can we dance
Whether you're a sail boat, a top hat or a dog,
Or a racing car taking it slow
Just remember to collect, your two hundred quid,
Every time that you pass go

The Woman on the Bus

I was sitting upstairs on a Number Eight bus
It was a little before 2 o' clock
Then a woman behind me, though it didn't surprise me
Took out her lunch in a box

She proceeded to take out her knife and fork
Not plastic mind you they were steel
Then she opened her map, laid it out on her lap
And sat there just eating a meal

That's when we heard her phone ringing
I say we cos the bus was quite packed
She let it ring twice, then in a very loud voice
She quickly went on the attack

Now of course we only heard her side
But she seemed to have him by the throat
It was something to do with a woman she knew
Some bloke and a twenty pound note

Well she switched off the phone in a paddy
She no longer wanted to talk
She slipped it back into her pocket
And dropped both her knife and her fork

She swore as she picked them both up off the floor
And went on to finish her lunch
Then all in a rush she pulled out her brush
And dragged her hair up in a bunch

Then she added a bit of mascara
And her lippy, just to be sure
But the point of this story, in all of it's glory
Is nothin' kept private no more ? ...

My Mind Wanders

You know when you're having a group conversation
And your mind wanders off on it's own
And you find yourself thinking about something more random
Like how quickly your toenails have grown

Or if they can put stripes in a tube of toothpaste
Why can't they make Tartan paint
And you realise you should have been listening
But the truth of it is that you ain't

Then you notice it's all gone quiet
And you figure they've asked you a question
So you try to remember the last thing you heard
While they're staring at your blank expression

A few seconds pass by really slowly
And you see this ain't going your way
And you don't want to sound like an ignorant git
But you can't think of nuthin' to say

So you jump up and just say "excuse me"
And make a quick dart for the loo
You hope by the time you get back you'll find
They've moved on to something new

And while you're in there you remember
No surely it wasn't a dream
It was something to do with Tartan toenails
But what could their question have been ? ...

I Went for a Walk down the Roman

I went for a walk down the Roman
Just for a quick look around
There wasn't a thing that I needed or wanted
But I still spent a couple of pound

I walked past the Pie and Mash shop
Well, when I say past, I walked in
"Two and Double of your finest please Luv"
And 7up out of a tin

Then once I was finished eating
I got up and left straight away
They don't mind you taking up space while you're eating
But they didn't invite me to stay

Then off I went down towards Costa
A tall skinny Latte to go
And back in the street to see who I'd meet
There'd usually be someone I know

I stopped for a chat with a girl from the flats
Who I knew back when I was a kid
And spoke to a bloke who was down on his luck
And left him a couple of quid

On to the stall that sells sweeties
For a quarter of Pineapple chunks
Sharing the sweets with some kids in the street
And sharing a joke with some drunks

…

...

Then a stroll to the end of the market
And looked in the window of Gregs
I didn't see anything that I really fancied
So I popped into Ingles instead

I picked up two fresh custard doughnuts
And phoned Mum to say I'd be round
I went for a walk down the Roman
Just for a quick look around

About a Million years Ago

About a million years ago,
when I was seventeen
We'd only just gone decimal
and pound notes were still green
Ernie was at number one,
the fastest Milkman in the west
Petrol was thirty five pence a gallon,
and we all drunk Courage Best

The world had lost The Beatles
and Leeds United won the cup
Nottingham Forest got relegated
and West Ham United stayed up
I had my first car, a Morris Minor,
and that car took me everywhere
Bowie was Ziggy Stardust
and I still had a full head of hair

I learned a lot about life that year,
what with one thing and the other
I heard Chuck Berry sing about My Ding a Ling
and Doctor Hook about Sylvia's Mother
My working life was under way,
and at last I had cash on the hip
I could take a girl out on a Saturday night,
and treat her to Wimpy and Chips

My bell bottom jeans had a thirty inch waist
and I didn't need glasses to read
Maybe naive, well enough to believe
that love really is all you need
My beard was a little bit darker then
and the future remained to be seen
About a million years ago, when I was seventeen

Bad Start

You know when you're having a bit of a bad day
And it ain't even started yet
You know that there's Coffee and Tea on offer
And you just don't know which one to get

You get up and look out the window
The sun's out and every thing's fine
But you know it will flippin' start raining
When your washing goes out on the line

You get in the shower and turn on the power
And then there's a knock at the door
So you turn off the power and get out of the shower
And there's water all over the floor

When you open the door it's the postman
With something you ordered on spec
You reach for a pen, to sign it and then
Wallop, your towel hits the deck

You can't tell your arse from your elbow
And you can't see the wood for the trees
You don't know if it's Friday or Pancake day
And whether to cough, fart or sneeze

Well that's how my Friday has started
Well some of it's true anyway
It's time to get on, well what else can go wrong
Famous last words as they say ...

Delayed at Almeria Airport

We're sitting here at Almeria airport
And they say there is a two hour flight delay
I'm guessing that the flight ain't yet left Stansted
I know they've had some problems there today

So I thought I'd grab a bite to eat while waiting
Just a sandwich or a bag of crisps
I queued up at the bar for twenty minutes
But wait now while you hear the best of this

The sandwiches they had were cheese and sausage
Or Serrano ham with spicy Spanish sauce
They also had a croissant with some jam or marmalade
And some cheese and onion Pringles too of course

So I chose the little cheese and sausage sandwich
And a tube of Pringles so I could be sure
A bottle of Coke Zero and then feeling like a hero
I asked the waiter Quanto es Señor ?

€16.60 .... ??

I hope we ain't delayed any longer ...lol...xx

Celebrity

Now, A listers go on the telly
And get interviewed by say, Graham Norton
Then others will go on that John Bishop show
Like Jo Brand or even James Corden

And then there are those who you don't really know
But they've been in some soap or another
Or somebody's mum who thought it was fun,
To go on Celebrity Big Brother

Then it becomes clear, that at this time of year,
There's one of two ways they can go
On one they make utter fools of themselves
And the other? You don't want to know

Australia sounds better than Blackpool
But it turns out it's raining in both
So it's eating a Kangaroo's danglies
Or treading on somebody's toes

Strictly or I'm a Celebrity,
Which one of them would you choose ?
Perhaps Ant and Dec or Anton du Beck
In a new pair of Black Patent shoes

Taking turns emptying the dunny
Or taking crap from Craig Revell Horwood
The Argentine Tango or sharing a Mango,
D'you know, I'm not sure that I could

Don't go out Without your Glasses

He was walking down the Roman when he saw her
And he'd swear to God he'd seen that walk before
But to tell the truth he wasn't wearing glasses
So in honesty he couldn't be too sure

He wondered if she might be in some television program
But for the life of him, he couldn't think which one
Her face looked so familiar but perhaps she just looked similar
To the girl who lived next door to his old Mum

Perhaps I went to school with her he wondered
But that was such a long long time ago
He followed when she went in Percy Ingles
But kept his distance, well you never know

He couldn't really see her very clearly
But something struck him as she turned her head
He thought she might have seen him so he stared up at the ceiling
As she turned back and chose a loaf of bread

She picked two Fresh Cream slices from the counter
But then she dropped her handbag on the floor
With a sudden flash of De ja vu, he wasn't sure what he should do
So he turned around and legged it out the door

Twenty years had passed now since he'd seen her
But the shiver down his spine remained for life
He's sure he won't go out without his glasses any more
He'd only nearly spoke to his ex wife

Facebook Groups and Cuppa Soups

Facebook Groups are like Cuppa Soups
They satisfy you for a short while
But when the fun's gone you have to move on
To find something that's more worthwhile

Someone does something that jangles your jubblies
Or you do something to them
You find you're no longer a part of that group
And it's let's go 'round again

If something affects you that strongly
Then pack up your keyboard and leave
Don't stay there arguing the toss with them
They'll believe what they want to believe

Nothing lasts forever because ..
nothing's meant to last
Whatever you see as the here and now
Is soon gonna be in the past

So whether you leave of your own volition
Or whether your kicked off a group
Don't take it to heart, just make a new start
And warm up a new Cuppa Soup

Ending too Soon (The Sixties)

When the hippies were heading to Woodstock
And Neil Armstrong walked on the moon
The Beatles played live on a rooftop in London
The Sixties were ending too soon

The age of Aquarius had dawned on us
And women's lib burst on the scene
Afghans and Kaftans and Adam West's Batman
And the Lemon Pipers Green Tambourine

We'd witnessed the birth of the mini skirt
And seen England win football's World cup
The kids had invented a passion for fashion
And everyone tried to keep up

The whole world had burst into colour
Led Zeppelin were Dazed and Confused
The Monkees had taken the Last Train to Clarksville
And Clapton was playing the blues

We'd seen the Berlin wall go up
But we'd live to see that come back down
Peace and Free Love, Ali's split glove
And The Stones had rolled into town

Martin Luther King had said I have a Dream
And hopefully opened our eyes
Dylan had told us The times they are changing
And Judy was in a disguise

James Bond was driving a new Aston Martin
And we all knew his signature tune
But when The Beatles played live on a rooftop in London
The Sixties were ending too soon

The New Season 2018
(West Ham United)

So that's it, we've spent all that money
And what have we got to show
A load of new players, that we've never heard of
And some that we think we should know

We've still got some ballast and make-weights
And some of our favourites remain
That's seven new players and three new shirts
And the manager's now whatsisname

I'm sure there'll be panic to start with
And we'll hear cries of "Off with his head"
But by Christmas if we are in seventh or eighth
He'll be the best thing since sliced bread

But here we are West Ham United
And we hope not united in grief
The Claret and Blue will always shine through
And as ever we'll keep our belief

That this season could be our season
I'm guessing top five is our aim
But we could finish sixth, seventh eighth ninth or tenth
Football's a funny old game

So let's keep on blowing our bubbles
And let them all hear when we sing
Manuel Pelligrini's claret and blue army ?
It does have a certain ring

Fish and Chips on Friday

Fish and Chips on Friday and some Orange squash to drink
Old school friends and fountain pens that covered you with ink
Being bored on Sundays and the old church hall bazaar
Boiled sweets and charcoal, helped to make us who we are

Rabbit stew and dumplings for an extra special treat
Playing in the summer rain with nothing on our feet
Climbing trees for conkers and a fire in the hearth
Boiling tubs of water to fill up the old tin bath

Sunday roast at 2 o'clock when your dad came from the pub
Your Mum down on her hands and knees, giving the doorstep a scrub
Knock down ginger, firework night and a sweet shop on the corner
The Cutty Sark and Greenwich park and watching the street performer

Chips and egg on Thursday and the shops all shut half day
Parties round your Nan's house when your cousins came to stay
Outside toilets, sculleries and a big old butler sink
Fish and Chips on Friday and some Orange squash to drink

I Got in a Little bit late Last night

I got in a little bit late last night
And the alcohol's fogging my brain
I had four pints of lager and some Gin and Tonics
I don't think I'll do that again

See, I went to a school reunion
In a pub down off Poplar high street
When you go on that trip along memory lane
You never know who you might meet

There were one or two people who knew me
And we soon all became the one crowd
There was dancing and singing and "Say that again"
And the music weren't half flippin' loud

We tried to recall some old stories
And some that we'd tried to forget
Do you remember, Oh what was her name?
And I still ain't remembered it yet

It was lovely to see some old faces
And to relive the days of our youth
We talked about all we remembered
Without fear or favour or proof

So God Bless ya, all who attended
I'm not gonna list all the names
'cos I got in a little bit late last night
And the alcohol's fogging my brain

I got out of the Shower this Morning

I got out of the shower this morning
And was standing there cleaning my teeth
The bath towel was wrapped round my midriff
And what happened next beggars belief

Now the window was slightly open
And the net curtain flapped in the breeze
I spotted my neighbour with the morning newspaper
Standing there waving at me

Now some things are done without thinking
So I casually waved back hello
But of course as I did, the knot, well undid
And that's when I felt the towel go

Well I dropped down as quick as the towel did
And ended up flat on the floor
My toothbrush went under the bathtub
And I then whacked my head on the door

I now found myself in a pickle
And felt that I had to explain
I got up too quick and flippin' well slipped
And wallop, I went down again

Then with all the dignity I could muster
I looked out the window and saw
The neighbour weren't waving at me after all
He was talking to the lady next door ...

I went out Without my Phone

I went out without my phone today
I left it plugged into the wall
What about if I'd had something to say
Or someone I wanted to call

I got home as quickly as possible
The world may have come to an end
What would I do if I missed something from you
And you were no longer my friend

But as it turned out I missed nothing
And luckily nobody died
But nobody could have got hold of me
But then again nobody tried

Nothing came through on the email
And the phone doesn't show a missed call
Facebook's remarkably quiet
And my Twitter feeds got bugger all

I admit that I panicked a little
'cos I thought that I'd dropped it, that's all
But when I got home, there was my phone
In the kitchen, plugged into the wall

So the moral of this if there is one
Is leave your phone home now and then
Because if nothing else, it's good for you health
And gets your blood pumping again

For Eileen

I looked into your eyes today and saw I wasn't there
You smiled because I smiled at you then hid behind a stare
You asked my name then asked again, a tiny recognition?
Gone as quickly as it came, no time for explanation

You just don't know me any more you're staring at my face
Through furrowed brow you try somehow to put things into place
I do my best to reassure you, we're the best of friends
You squeeze my hand and then you ask me who I am again

Your mem'ry has abandoned me it wasn't through your choice
My face means nothing to you, you don't recognise my voice
But I still know who you are, and while life will play its part
I'll sit and hold your hand and hold you ever in my heart

Foreign Exchange

The beds are all made, I've emptied the fridge
And we've been to the foreign exchange
We've changed up some money and some of it's funny
And some of it looks rather strange

"This time next year", I told Mary once
"We will be Millionaires"
Now here we are, with five point eight million
And somehow it seems she don't care

Admittedly it's 5.8 million Rupiah
And we're going to spend it in Bali
But as has been said, It's three hundred quid
So I'm not going to buy a Ferrari

Three thousand Eight hundred Hong Kong Dollars
I'm starting to feel pretty rich
Six hundred and eighteen, Singapore Dollars
Perhaps it is time for a switch

Of course we'll be taking our Credit Cards
And I'm sure they will too have their say
So for now I'll say "See Ya", and "Wouldn't want to be Ya"
We're going on our Holiday

Growing up in the 50s and 60s

Growing up in the 50s and 60s
We know was the greatest of times
Kids today don't know that they're born
They don't even eat chocolate limes

They don't know the joy of a debris
Or to play in a row of bombed houses
Or walking to school on a freezing cold morning
In ankle high sock and short trousers

They ain't even heard of cough candy
And Cream soda has gone out of fashion
It's true that they do like a cup of Typhoo
But somehow they don't share our passion

They won't even try bread and dripping
And they don't know what Sunday Best means
Look at them now with their iPhones and Androids
Though they do still have holes in their jeans

They laugh when they ask 'bout the old days
And we laugh at the way that they speak
Their eyes just glaze over and they say Yeah, whatever
When we tell them what we earned a week

...

...

Our pop music came from the pirates
And recorded on a cassette machine
Theirs is downloaded from iTunes or You tube
With no DJ's voice in between

The Beatles gave way to the Beat Box
While the Rappers come up with the rhymes
Growing up in the 50s and 60s
My favourites were Chocolate Limes

Proper Pie and Mash
(Traditional East End Pie and Mash)

We parked down Barking road today and felt a little hungry
I didn't fancy burger and chips and didn't want a curry
But there it was just sitting there and cutting quite a dash
A proper Pie 'n' Mash shop selling proper Pie 'n' Mash

Two and double and Two and double for not a lot of dosh
Liquor, pepper and loads of vinegar and a glass of orange squash
Football on the telly and a shrine to Bobby Moore
Loads of room and a fork and spoon, who could ask for more

I strongly recommend it if your heading down that way
Tell 'em Chris and Mary sent you, we were there today
Good Luck to them In Barking Road I hope they make a splash
A proper Pie 'n' Mash shop, Selling proper Pie 'n' Mash

I Forgot

I forgot to take my shopping list to Asda
I forgot what I had written on the list
But as I didn't bring it, I decided I would wing it
And check it later, to see what I had missed

It seems that I forgot to get the Salmon
So the Salmon Pasta Bake will have to wait
I didn't get the Chocolate Biscuits either
But never mind, I'm trying to lose some weight

I didn't get the Onions and forgot the Ragu sauce
And forgot the mincemeat had to be defrosted
So I'll wait a few more days until I do the Bolognese
And it seems that I forgot the Kellogg's Frosties

I didn't do the Lottery and not 'cos I forgot you see
I thought I'd do it as I left the store
But by the time I got to grips with buying my two Lucky Dips
The queue was right out past the swinging door

I forgot to get potatoes so I'll have to get them later
And the carrots and the pizza and the peas
It seems that we've run out of Piccalilli
And marmalade for breakfast if you please

I forgot to get the Bisto and the sweetcorn
And more importantly forgot the wine
So I'm going round the Savacentre to see if I do any better
And make sure that I take my list this time

Heroes and Villains

Life's full of Heroes and Villains
And somehow we all choose our own
Those we dislike with a hate at first sight
And those that we'd like to have known

You see someone come on the telly
And you think, oh I can't stand this bloke
Or that girl on that show that you don't really know
But you think someone's having a joke

And we don't always like the same people
And that's what I don't understand
Somebody points out their favourite celeb
And it's somebody that you can't stand

There don't seem to be rhyme or reason
But it seems that don't matter a jot
We don't see their potential cos we're all so judgemental
We don't like them and bosh, that's their lot

Then there's your favourite singer
Who you think has a fantastic voice
And your mate thinks he sounds like a pack of wolf hounds
I guess it's all personal choice

Now I don't want to make this too negative
And name anyone personally
But I can't stand that bloke who does poems on Facebook
Oh no, wait a minute, that's me

I Once looked like One of the Bee Gees

I once looked like one of the Bee Gees
With my long hair and pants way to tight
I'd wear my shirt slashed to the navel
Wherever I went day or night

A big gold identity bracelet
And a medallion hung on a chain
It used to just rest on the hair on my chest
But that was just part of the game

I once looked like one of the Bee Gees
And not the good looking one either
But good looking enough to go strutting my stuff
When it came to the Saturday Night Fever

Lookin' back it was a Tragedy
Though we did what we did to survive
But nobody got Too much Heaven back then
And it was all about Stayin' Alive

Now that was all back in the seventies
And everything has to move on
The hair and the shirts and medallion
Tight pants and the bracelet are gone

And now I look more like Alf Garnett
With my bald head and glasses as well
But I once looked like one of the Bee Gees
If you look closely, perhaps you can tell ??

I just Wish it would Flippin' Slow Down

We used to go to Walthamstow
To watch the dogs run round
They've left the façade and a bit of the yard
But they closed the Dog track down

We used to go to Upton Park
To watch the Hammers play
But the Boleyn Ground is no longer around
They've moved down toward Stratford way

The Speedway on Hackney Marshes
And the Odeon there at Mile End
The Municipal baths at Stepney Green
We won't step inside them again

Woolworth's has gone out of business
And who knows where Rumbelow's went
The room at the Top and Top of the Pops
Pound Notes and Shillings and Pence

They knocked down the school that I went to
And a new one was built in its place
The pub on the corner is a small block of flats
My world seems to wear a new face

...

...

In my life I've seen lots of changes
And we've lost lots of things that we had
But I'm still here breathing and you're still there reading
So let's face it, it can't be all bad

The Lido has gone from Victoria park
And the Royal Mint moved out of town
I know it ain't strange and that things have to change
I just wish it would flipping' slow down

Canary Wharf

I used to live on the Isle of Dogs
Before it was what it is now
We lived in a flat on Samuda Estate
Before the Docklands went all highbrow

A long time before the new DLR
And the office blocks reaching the heavens
When the only way off and back on to the island
Was to drive or the 277

The Blue bridge was always a nightmare,
And the swing-bridge, a little bit tight
The docks were still open and the dockers still hoping
The unions would fight the good fight

From Glengall Road school to the Millwall dock wall
From the Mudchute to Tiller Road baths
The City Pride was round the far side
And Thermopylae gate made me laugh

The launch site of Brunel's Great Eastern
The foot tunnel under the Thames
Some things don't change and some things seem strange
And some things just come round again

We watched as they built the Dockland Arena
Sinatra appeared in there once
We watched as they knocked down the Docklands Arena
I don't think they gave it a chance

...

...

I'd moved out before the yuppies moved in
But the island was no longer mine
The docks didn't last and it happened so fast
That Canary wharf hit the skyline

I have to say though I still love it
It's just like Manhattan on Thames
And given a chance and a six figure advance
I'd go back and live there again

Ironing

I'm not much of one for the ironing
It just isn't what I do best
I'm alright with Tea Towels and Pillow slips
And my boxers and perhaps the odd vest

Flat sheets and Flannels are easy
And jeans are okay I suppose
But next time that I go to Lakeside
I'm buying some non iron clothes

I ain't got the patience for ironing a shirt
It ends up more creased than it starts
I find that I leave, at least one of the sleeves
And it's worse when the back has those darts

Tee shirts that have to be done inside out
And the ones with the collars are worse
But there's one little treat that has everything beat
It's known as the ironing day curse

The double size, deep fitted valance sheet
You can't fit that thing on your board
And the valance has pleats and you can't keep them neat
When it wraps round the electrical cord

See I'm alright with Shopping and cooking
And dusting and all of the rest
But I'm not much of one for the ironing
It just isn't what I do best

Leonora Babitov
(Facebook Friend Request)

I got a friend request from Leonara Babitov
A lovely girl she looked as well with most of her clothes off
Offering me services that quite frankly made me blush
I quickly flicked through her profile pics in a rather hasty rush

Does everybody get these things or is it only me
Yesterday I got two more and this morning I got three
Evidently I'm the one they've all been searching for
Well ladies I can only say you'd better search some more

All you need and want from me is that I'm sending fare
And then you'll fly to Gatquick
And you'll call when you get there
You say you want to married me and came to London soon
I did ask Mary what she thought but she said we ain't got room

You tell me that you're twenty three and you like older men
I'll have to put my glasses on and read that bit again
To be honest I'm a little bit skint right now and I have been ever since
I sent my bank details and stuff to a friendly Nigerian Prince

So God bless you Leonora now your story has been told
I have to say that you have made a happy man very old
But alas I must turn down your offer
And I've deleted your friend request
I've already had one heart attack and I think it's for the best

London (There's No Place like Home)

Born and Raised in London and I've lived there all my life
It's where I went to primary school and where I met my wife
Although her family's Irish she's from London too
Through a passageway from Galway Bay
We're London through and through

It's where I first had Pie and Mash and Spaghetti Bolognese
I've travelled far but the chances are it's where I'll end my days
We could move to the country or a bungalow by the sea
But I'm still part of London just as London's part of me

Now travel is our passion and we love to chase the sun
We've been around the world a bit but we ain't nearly done
We've been to Spain and Washington,
Las Vegas and New York
Florida and Singapore, Greece, Hong Kong and Cork

Hawaii and Los Angeles, Portugal and Crete,
Milan and San Francisco where we partied in the street
We took a chance and went to France
And a week on a beach in Corfu
Majorca, Minorca and Bali, and Berlin and Denmark too

But London's where we come from and London's who we are
Trafalgar Square, the Palaces, or a Soho coffee bar
The Tower and the Theatres and St. Paul's Cathedral's dome
Big Ben's clock and the poshed up docks,
There is no place like home

Nothing Tastes as Good as you Remember

Nothing tastes as good as you remember
Like Chocolate Limes or even Caramac
Tizer will surprise ya and just as an advisor
If you pick up Sherbet Lemons, put them back

Nothing lasts as long as you remember
Like holidays and Sunday afternoons
Weekends pass by in a flash along with all your spending cash
And Mondays seem to come around too soon

Nothing is as big as you remember
Like Yorkie or a stick of seaside rock
Remember when you couldn't fit a Creme Egg in your mouth ?
And a Wagon Wheel was the size of Big Ben's clock

Nothing's even called what you remember
Like Peanut Treets and even Opal fruits
Marathon is long since gone and I could just go on and on
But really it's no wonder we're confused

Perhaps then we were smaller and perhaps the world was taller
and perhaps it's that our memories are shot
But with changing tastes and compromises,
things in different shapes and sizes
Our memories are all we've flippin' got

The Seventies (2)

When I think of the nineteen seventies
A few things come back to my mind
Some things we brought along with us
And some things that we left behind

The patchwork suede jackets with big roundy collars
In two shades of Blue, Brown or Mauve
The Morris Marinas and Mk 3 Cortinas
And Volkswagen Beetles we drove

Diana Ross at the cinema
The Lady sings the Blues
Marc Bolan trying to Ride a white swan
And Elton John's huge platform shoes

Charlies Angels and big plastic bangles
Blue Nun and Gilbert O'Sullivan
Nixon's Whitewash, Tree Top fruit squash
Columbo and Dana and Donovan

Soap on a rope and living in hope
Of a boil in the bag curry for two
Linda Lewis singing "It's in his kiss"
And Rocking her doodle doo

When Lennon imagined no heaven
And the rest of the world sang along
Lulu wore black velvet hot pants
And then we all knew he was wrong

Some Mothers do 'ave 'em on telly
And The last of the Summer Wine
Just some things we brought along with us
And some things that we left behind

The Speed Awareness Course

Well it seems that I got nicked for speeding again
And the people from law enforcement
Offered a Speed Awareness Course
Or a fine and another endorsement

While my points tally isn't too scary
Another three wasn't my aim
So I went on the Speed Awareness Course
And I took the walk of shame

They told us the dangers of speeding
And how even a little's a lot
How Forty is Naughty and Twenty is Plenty
No matter what car you've got

They asked us a few basic questions
And tested us on reading the signs
Like how do you know there's a hazard approaching
By looking down at the white lines

How can you tell the speed limit they asked
On a street that ain't got any signs
I knew the answer to that one though
'cos the truth is this ain't my first time

I completed my act of contrition
I joined in and gave of my best
I was a bit scared in case somebody dared
To ask me to resit my test

But I listened and took in the message
And the truth is you know it makes sense
Or at least be a bit more observant
When the speed camera's just by the fence

Thursday was Half Day Closing

Thursday was half day closing,
And on Fridays we'd get in the bath
Saturday Morning we'd wash my Dad's car
And then go to West Ham for a laugh

Sunday meant New Zealand lamb for our dinner
And cockles with pepper for tea
Sunday Night at the London Palladium
Upstairs on my Nan's old settee

Monday Morning walking to school
Like every day of the week
Then left over meat from the Sunday roast
With a nice bit of bubble and squeak

Tuesdays were always quite special
And sometimes we'd have Pie and Mash
But only if Mum could afford it that week
If not then she'd make Corned Beef hash

Wednesday was always washing day
And our Mum would uncover the mangle
I'd feed the clothes through, one by one
While my Brother was turning the handle

We knew where we were back in them days
And them days set us on the right path
Thursday was half day closing,
And on Fridays we'd get in the bath

Painkillers

You know when you're taking pain killers
For say maybe you've broken your toe
You whack in a couple of Ibuprofen
How do they know where to go?

Now some people take them for headaches
And some 'cos they've got a bad back
Sometimes you might have a shoulder that's hurting
But they always know where to attack

See I don't take painkillers that often
But I did take a course in September
For a pain in my arm and they worked like a charm
But I'm worried that they might remember

How will they know it's my left leg this time
And the pain in the arm is now fine
I don't want them going lookin' for trouble
You never know what they might find

Perhaps the best bet is to tell 'em
Just so they know what to do
Okay boys, It's the left hip today
Good luck, we're relying on you

Or is it just all an illusion
An old fashioned medicine show
You know when you're taking painkillers
How do they know where to go

Armrests

Who owns the rights to the armrests,
when you sit in an aeroplane seat
There's three seats but there are four armrests,
so the spare one's a bit of a treat

If the bloke in the middle takes one either side
the other two only get one
But if the girl on the aisle and the one by the window
take two then the middle gets none

Now the person who sits by the window,
and the one who sits two seats away
Have one either side that they don't need to hide,
as they're obviously theirs anyway

While the window seat has its advantages
and the aisle seat can cause less frustration
Perhaps the middle seat should get the armrests,
as a "Drew the short straw" compensation

It's all a bit of a minefield
and nobody knows where they stand
And when someone gets up to go to the loo,
it can all get a bit out of hand

Is it first come first served ? Should I be this concerned ?
I don't like admitting defeat
But who owns the rights to the armrests,
when you sit in an aeroplane seat

Homeless

If you don't want to give me some money
And you don't want to give me a hand
If you want to walk by with your eyes to the sky
Don't worry mate, I understand

'cos I haven't always been homeless
I used to be where you are now
But life ran away and suffice it to say
It ran away from me somehow

I've heard all the arguments about it
And maybe I've said some myself
"Why don't you get up and go get a job ?"
"You're not even helping yourself"

Well the truth is job searching ain't easy
It's just like the Chicken and Egg
You can't get a job, without an address
But trust me no one wants to beg

Now, if you do want to help me
With a couple of quid and a smile
Or that coat you don't wear, or the boots you have spare
That might keep me warm for a while

A scarf or a hat, or something like that
Believe me, this ain't what I planned
But, if you want to walk by, with your eyes to the sky
Don't worry mate ... I understand

Humour

What ever happened to humour ?
D'you remember telling a joke ?
About someone's wife or Mother in Law
Or about some fat bald headed bloke

The Englishman, Irishman and Scotsman
Don't go in the pub any more
And no one's allowed to tell jokes in a crowd
Without being slung out the door

Gone are the days of I say I say I say
'cos we never know what's coming next
But it's bound to be Racist or Sexist or Ageist
And somebody's gonna get vexed

We can't tell the jokes that we used to
In case someone else gets offended
So when it comes to blondes and Essex girls
It seems it's least said soonest mended

There were two Jewish guys in a Sauna
But I can't tell the rest of that story
And the one about Archbishop Tutu
Is certain to cause a furore

When did we all get so touchy
And perhaps we could go back somehow
I heard a right Brahma about Barak Obama
And I can't even tell that one now

EastEnders

I've never been to Albert Square
And I never met Den or Angie
I never stood in the Queen Vic bar
And drunk a lager shandy

I never had my Bacon rolls
Served up by Kathy Beale
I never did see that Walford FC
But I heard they beat Tottenham three nil

Now I've never seen, Pat or Pauline
I don't know Sharon or Grant
I thought I might go to the Launderette though
But I found out the truth is I can't

But I promise I am an Eastender
I could wear a Pearly King's crown
All Pie and Mash and Corned beef hash
And knees up Muvver Brown

Mile End Station and self preservation
The Beggars and Petticoat lane
Bethnal Green Road and an East End postcode
West Ham and some Rhyming slang

Now I know that I sound like Frank Butcher
But that's just the way that I speak
And if you want to see, some more about me
You'll just have to tune in next week

Bethnal Green Road

As I walk through the underground station
I come out by the Salmon and Ball
'cos you can't get the train down as far as Brick Lane
So I'll get on the bus or just walk

But walking brings back many memories
Of how Bethnal Green used to be
The pubs where we'd go and the people we'd know
And familiar faces we'd see

For a start the Salmon was Tipples
Then the nick has moved on somewhere else
The Camden's is now called The Bethnal Green Tavern
They've got the smell of them self

The coach station turned into Kwik Fit
And the White Hart has changed its name too
It's now called The Star of Bethnal Green
I'm not sure if anyone knew

The wallpaper shop has closed down too
But we still have all those market stalls
There's two Pie and Mash shops,
Some number eight bus stops
And Attenborough's three big brass balls

...

...

The Greengate's a food supermarket
So we won't go in that pub again
So much has changed but a lot's still the same
As I'm getting close now to Brick Lane

And then I am stood at the traffic lights
I can see from there what I came for
The gateway to heaven, 'cos twenty four seven
There's no locks on the Biegel Shop door

Cleaning the Bathroom

When it comes to cleaning your bathroom
I've got a quick question to ask
Do you start to clean, when you first walk in
Or after your shower or bath?

There's two sides to every story
And I'm sure that you know what I mean
If you polish the glass, then shower or bath
There'll be marks left to show where you've been

Your taps won't then be quite as shiny
And your vitreous china won't gleam
You'll give them a wipe, and they may look alright
But things aren't always as they seem

But if you get in the shower first
And ev'rything's then soaking wet
When you start to clean into places unseen
You know that you'll soon break a sweat

And then of course you'll need a shower
But the floor's wet so mind where you tread
Or just have your shower, go out for an hour
And do housework tomorrow instead ...

God's Gifts

When the Good Lord created yours truly
He gave me a few special gifts
Some of which I won't go into right now
And some which I'll try now to list

He started, of course, with my parents
A proper good choice from the start
He gave me a voice that could carry a tune
And I like to think a kind heart

Two ears and a love of good music
Though my eyesight ain't what it could be
My hair all fell out, now what's that about
But these are the things that make me

He gave me a fair sense of humour
And the knowledge to know when I'm beat
His words still ring true, in most things I do
And his last words to me I'll repeat

To brighten your life even further
You'll marry an Irishman's Daughter
But to make sure you don't get too carried away
I'll make you a West Ham supporter

Him off the Telly

You know when you're watching the telly
And someone comes on who you know
I don't mean you know him in real life
But you've seen him in some other show

And you say to the wife, "look who that is"
And she looks at you like you're mad
"I've never seen him before in my life"
But you're 100% sure that you had

He was in that programme with what's her name
Who's now in that programme we like
You know the woman, the one with the glasses
Who's on on a Saturday night

That ain't him, your Mrs says
He didn't talk like that
Of course it's him you tell her
But he used to wear a hat

He was an awful lot younger mind you
And his hair colour wasn't the same
I think that he played a policeman
Oh bugger me what is his name
...

...

Why don't you check it on Google
No, I know it will come to me soon
You know that you'll check it on Google
As soon as your wife leaves the room

So you give in and fire up the laptop
And search what the internet knows
It turns out it wasn't him after all
It didn't half look like him though

I Can't Keep on top of The Washing

Now these days I do lots of jobs 'round the house
And that's just the way it should be
Mary still goes out to work everyday
So the housework has fallen to me

The hoovering and dusting is easy
And I quite like the cooking and shopping
And making the bed but it has to be said
I can't keep on top of the washing

I feel like I'm running a Chinese laundry
And the washing machine's taking the strain
As soon as the clothes horse is empty
The basket is full up again

I think Mary's taking in washing
Cos I don't wear that many clothes
Though I recognise most of the tee shirts
And I've worn most of them I suppose

Then there's the socks and the whassnames
But we won't mention them in this rhyme
Mary's work dresses and all she possesses
Keep coming round time after time

Of course there's the towels and the bedsheets
It seems to go on without stopping
With all of the things that the ev'ryday brings
I can't keep on top of the washing

Biscuits

Now when it comes to biscuits, I'm an expert
It's a wonder that I'm in the shape I'm in
I do like two or three, when I have a cup of tea
And I keep a nice selection in my tin

For me a Custard Cream's the best for dunking
With Scottish Shortbread just in second place
I like the ones with flies in and there's really no disguising
That extra special chocolate Bourbon taste

Now of course you've got your Jaffa Cakes and Hob Nobs
Jammie Dodgers, Nice and Malted Milk
I like a Garibaldi and a Chunky Chocolate Cookie
And those Choco Leibniz taste as smooth as silk

I once went out and bought a pack of Viscounts
And they went down a treat with both the girls
But as for them Fig Rolls, well, I really ain't that old
But I love those Mr Kiplings Viennese Whirls

Now all these fade away as if to nothing
When a glass of ice cold milk has been suggested
'cos as I've said and as you've read, at night before I go to bed
You just can't beat a Dark Chocolate Digestive ...

...or two

Morning Aerobics

I just done my morning aerobics
When I went out and got into the car
A spider decided, although uninvited
To spin his web shaped like a star

Now the truth is that I wasn't looking
I just got in the way that you do
Then I felt something here at the back of my ear
And realised what I'd just walked through

Well I started with flicking my ear lobe
Then both ears and the top of my head
But that just made it worse so I let out a curse
I won't tell you here what I said

I opened the door and jumped out on the floor
And that was the start of the action
I pulled my shirt off and was starting to cough
As I danced like a young Michael Jackson

I was whirling around like a dervish
And flicking myself with my shirt
The way I was moving and shaking and grooving
It's a wonder that no one got hurt

Mary was laughing her head off
And it must have looked pretty bizarre
But before very long I put my shirt on
And then stepped back into the car

Then I dropped Mary off at the station
And although I'm not arachnaphobic
That spider's still out there, In the car somewhere
But I've done do my Morning aerobics

Sisters

Do you remember Sissy, when we were seventeen ?
Dancing up the Palais and all the things we've seen
Coffee bars and Movie stars, Teddy boys and girls
Trams and queues and Pathe news, a new twin set and pearls

Nylon stockings, up town shopping and freezing when it snowed
The day I met my Arthur, on a bus on Mile End Road
Sitting 'round the fireplace in our old nan's front room
And listening to the wireless on Sunday afternoon

And do you remember Ada, in that dress that our Mum made ya
When you tripped the light fantastic with that yank
And how we stood and cried that day, while listening to Johnny Ray
As his ship sailed out and your heart sank

Holding hands and making plans and walking in the park
Making sure that you were home before it got too dark
Fog and Smog and barking dogs and Bobbies on the beat
But now we sit here on this bench to rest our aching feet

Have things changed for the better ?, I'm afraid I don't know dear
But every day, in every way, we see the changes here
There's girls out in pyjamas and in ripped and ragged jeans
We'd never go out dressed like that, when we were seventeen

Old Shirt

I'm wearing this shirt for the last time today
The wife says that it has to go
I've had it so long that the colour has gone
And the front of it's got a small hole

And also it's kinda misshapen
And don't fit like it did back then
There are one or two stains and the Mrs complains
When she irons it time and again

But I have to say that it's my favourite
And has been for quite a long time
I bought it in Walgreens in Orlando in Florida
Back in Two thousand and Nine

I took it when we went to Bali
And I wore it when we went to Spain
In Savannah and Crete and on Carnaby St.
And back to Orlando again

But perhaps Mary's right and it's over
And perhaps now it's time it was gone
I couldn't go out in the street in it now
But to throw it away just seems wrong

Maybe I'll wash it and take it upstairs
And hide it in one of the drawers
And the hole could be sewn and when I'm on my own
I could maybe just wear it indoors

Until Next Time
By Tiernie Jayne Ross, Poppy-Lilly Ross (and Grandad)

On the first of August, we were round our Grandad's house
Nanny went out early but was quiet as a mouse
Later in the morning Grandad jumped onto our bed
"Come on you two", "get up now", "It's breakfast time", he said

So down we went, he made the tea, and poured it out for us
He made us both some Weetabix, we didn't make a fuss
We went into the garden with our water pistols out
We both squirted our Grandad, you should have heard him shout

We went upstairs and had a bath with bubbles and shampoo
And then we came down stairs again and wrote this verse for you
We had some help from Grandad as we wrote this little rhyme
We're going home today and we cant wait until next time

Selfies

There's a girl in the bar taking selfies
And she's got everybody's attention
Now I like a selfie as much as the next bloke
But there's one or two things I should mention

She's taken about 650 so far
Hair down and then up in a bun
Sunglasses on and Sunglasses off
While there's no flippin' sign of the Sun

First smiling then posing then pouting
Some up highs and then some down lows
I think that last one may have been a mistake
The camera saw right up her nose

When you go through them all for the best one
It don't matter which one you choose
The chances are when your done posing
They all pretty much look like you

I wonder what she'll do with these pictures
And why she's sat there on her own
Is she out on a date or out with her mate
Or is it just her and her phone

Oh I see there's her bloke's getting drinks in
And he's flippin' doing it now
I'm sure that they get it together tonight
And Snapchat each other somehow

Ten Years Younger

I tend to look bigger in photos
And sometimes I even look bald
Is this a new photographic phenomenon
And if so, d'you know what it's called

'cos I don't look like that in the mirror
I look like I did years ago
Oh well alright, my shirt's a bit tight
And my hairline's beginning to go

I've still got the old fashioned six pack
With maybe a couple to spare
I know I look good in my speedo
By the way that the ladies still stare

But I line up to be in a picture
Then someone starts having a joke
I get displaced and then get replaced
By some big old fat baldy bloke

Personally I blame Adobe
It's their Photoshop app that's to blame
We all used to cry, the camera don't lie
But nowadays things ain't the same

So if you see pictures on Facebook
There's something I have to confess
In real life I look ten years younger
And weigh at least two and half stone less

The Bestest Day Ever

The train now standing at platform three
Will soon be heading out, down to the sea
The first stop is Ilford, and Romford and then
Every station along to Southend

Slam shut doors, and corridors too
Guards checking tickets, as they pass through
Drop down windows, and games to play
Mum's taking us to the seaside today

Off at the station and over the road
Onto the beach, all sharing the load
Towels and sandwiches, buckets and spades
Setting up camp near the penny arcades

Swimming and splashing and building sand castles
Running and jumping and digging for cockles
Mum coming down to the edge for a paddle
She says it's too cold as it splashes her ankles

Stones in my cozzie and sand in my ears
Candy Floss, slot machines and one or two tears
A fish and chip supper as the street lights come on
Full up and tired, it's time to go home

Now the day's over and back on the train
Falling asleep bound for London again
The bestest day ever and so full of fun
Can we do it again, really soon? ... Can we Mum ? ...xx

The Kiddies Section

We sat in the kiddies section
On the flight coming back home from Spain
After a two and a half hour delay at the airport
And in truth I don't want to complain

But when you've got a kid sitting behind you
And he gives the tray table a whack
It bounces about a couple of times
And vibrates right up through your back

The children in front have an iPad
I think it belongs to their Dad
They're both watching something called Pitch perfect 3
With no headphones on I might add

It's my own fault I know, not the children
They don't know I'm trying to sleep
Or the fact I don't care about Paddington Bear
Or the wool from the Baa Baa black sheep

But when you hear the words , Mum, are we there yet ?
And sit down Johnny seventeen times
Daddy, I need to go to the toilet
And then little Amy starts crying'

It gets a bit, shall we say wearing
I don't think I'll book those seats again
But who knew that there was a kiddies section
On the flight coming back home from Spain

The Fox

My street door opens into my living room
And the stairs are there as you come past
I lay out this plan so that you understand
What happened the night before last

Now we do tend have the door open
Though nothing or no one comes in
So we're not always paying attention
And that's where our story begins

Well, I was sitting here watching the telly
And Mary was sat there with me
I was caught unawares when I glanced at the stairs
And a Fox stood there staring at me

He must have been upstairs exploring
After strolling in sometime before
He came down the stairs and stood there and stared
Then turned left to go out of the door

But the door had blown shut when he got there
So he turned and ran back up the stairs
It was just like a dream, Mary let out a scream
And I guess we were both a bit scared

...

...

So I followed him up to the landing
Keeping my back to the wall
I didn't know what I would do when I got there
But couldn't do nothing at all

Then just like they do on the telly
With with my fingers shaped into a gun
I entered the bathroom and into the bedrooms
And closed all the doors, one by one

Well I soon found out where he was hiding
And was feeling a little bit vexed
So I came back downstairs to my laptop
And asked Google what I should do next

I opened the door, just in case like before,
He came down to let himself out
As Google had nothing to offer
I thought I was in with a shout

And then he appeared on the staircase
And looked at me straight in the eye
As we stared at each other, one step after the other
And he left without saying goodbye

Git ...lol

The NHS

I was born on the NHS
Cost my mum nothing, except pain and stress
They took out my tonsils and most of my teeth
All done with love and with care and belief

It got me through childhood, with coughs colds and flu
Fractures and stitches and new glasses too
Eye operations and when I got run over
They booked me in hospital for a two night stopover

They took care of my Mum, when she broke her hip
They gave her a new one and gave her a stick
Paid for in taxes but not at the door
Same succour and comfort for rich and for poor

Births Deaths and X-rays, they kept us on track
And then came the big one, a full Heart Attack
The treatment I got was just simply the best
Alive and surviving a Cardiac Arrest

The Nurses and Doctors the best anywhere
No better treatment, No better care
They may have their problems but nevertheless
I wouldn't be here without our NHS

Yesterday once More

If only our youth hadn't left us
And the telly was still black and white
If we just had the strength and desire
To go out and to stay out all night

If only tomorrow was yesterday,
Or even the weekend before
If my age still started with a two or a three
Or for that matter even a four

If the music hadn't gone Hip Hop
And we still knew the words to the songs
If things hadn't changed quite as quickly
And we found all our knowledge was wrong

If only the past was the future
If we could just unlock that door
If we could just turn back the hands of time
But then again I'm not so sure

'cos we'd all be indoors watching Dallas
And worried about who shot JR
WiFi would turn back to HiFi
And Max Bygraves would still be a star

We wouldn't have Facebook or Laptops
No mobiles but the no Geordie Shore
But when I sing along to the Carpenters song
I do wish it was Yesterday once more

Global Warming ?

I was just outside pegging out washing
While whistling a happy tune
And then I remembered that we're in September
With weather that feels more like June

The garden's not covered with leaves from the trees
And Autumn has been put on hold
I'm still wearing shorts and a tee shirt
And not even feeling the cold

Is this it ? Is this global warming?
Does this mean we're all gonna die
If that is the case for the whole human race
I thought that I'd best say goodbye

'cos we're going on holiday on Saturday
And if the world should end while we're away
There's a few things that I'd like to get off of my chest
And a few things that I'd like to say

But what if I upset some people
And what if the world doesn't end
I'll be all on my own but still having a moan
But this time without any friends

So perhaps I should keep my own council
And keep all my thoughts to myself
'cos I don't want to find that I've been left behind
Or my books to be left on the shelf

I'm sure it's an Indian Summer
And I've just had a panic attack
But we're still going on holiday on Saturday
And I hope you're here when we get back

Super Glue

I bought a tube of super glue to fix my reading glasses
that I sat on while on holiday in Spain
I've never really had much luck, when gluing stuff that's come unstuck
but thought the time had come to try again

So I bought the glue from B&Q, a special offer pack of two,
and read all the instructions on the back
And spent the next half hour or so, swearing at the so and so
and trying to get the tube out of the pack

Well I got the cap off of the thing and went and got a safety pin,
and poked it through and broke the metal seal
Feeling happy with myself, I got the glasses off the shelf
and put the pin down on the window sill

Now it seems I hadn't noticed yet, the safety pin was slightly wet
and by this time was stuck fast where it lay
I couldn't stop to free it now my hands were full and anyhow,
the job I came to do was under way

So I squirted out a glob of glue, it seems though that I'd squirted two
and a little bit fell by the kitchen door
The pin was still stuck to the whatsername,
my finger got stuck to the glasses frame
and the sole of my slipper got stuck to the laminate floor

The glasses didn't stick of course but face it now it could be worse,
they could have wound up sticking to my face
So I took the glasses and the glue and the
packaging it came in too
And put them in my Man Draw ... Just in case

Goodbye Mike
(Requiem for a Friend)

I'll say a short prayer for an old friend tonight
Who's passed from the darkness and into the light
We'll both shed a tear at the thought that you're gone
But mem'ries of friendship will go on and on

I just can't believe we won't see you again
And laugh as we run from the Florida rain
You touched us in ways that you can't understand
Since the day we first met on Montego Bay's sand

You made us your family and we made you ours
We sat and we chatted for hours and hours
With Katie and Mary, the four musketeers
I know you'll excuse and forgive us our tears

Go on in peace and with God's holy grace
We'll miss you but keep you and love you no less
Goodbye my old friend you will stay with us yet
In spirit and love, we will never forget

God Bless Mike ...xx

I Made Myself

I made myself a cup of tea this morning
And I have to say it's going down a treat
I made a Lemon Drizzle cake on Sunday
And there's still a bit of that there left to eat

Mary took the rest to work this morning
To share among her colleagues, as you do
Now, the bit I had last night was tangy, sweet and light
But I'll wait 'til later on for the reviews

I made myself get out of bed this morning
And got Mary to the station just in time
I made some toast and marmalade for breakfast
And I eat it while I sat and wrote this rhyme

I might make a Lasagne for our dinner
A winter favourite long since well rehearsed
I'll pop along to Asda for some flat lasagne pasta
But I'll have another cup of Typhoo first

I wrote this little story as I sat and drunk my tea
To greet you all this morning as you wake
And let you know what's going on in my house
And get my mind off Lemon Drizzle cake

Southend on Sea

What a day we had today,
down there at Southend on Sea
Tiernie Jayne, Poppy Lily,
and of course there was Mary and me

Swimming in the estuary,
And sunbathing out on the stones
As I was brought up in the East End of London
This really is my second home

Hot Dogs with onions and pink burger relish,
Washed down with a cold can of Coke
Watching the kids as they splashed in the fountain,
While we spoke to some Latvian bloke

Putting some pennies in slot machines
In a place called the "Monte Carlo"
Trust me if you've got some money to waste
There's no place better you can go

Hot Sugar Donuts, to finish the day
With a bottle of this or that pop
Make sure the girls have all been to the Ladies, '
'cos you know there'll be nowhere to stop

Watching them doze in the back of the car,
It's alright for them but not me
What a day we had today,
Down there at Southend on Sea

Fast Food Diet

I was just walking by, when a sign caught my eye
And the words stopped me dead in my tracks
No, that can't be right ? ... so I thought that I might,
Have another look, so I went back

And there it was, plain as the nose on your face
The words we've been longing to hear
There's a new diet out, and guess what it's about?
Yep, Cream cakes and Burgers and Beer

It seems you can eat all the fast food you want
And not even put on an ounce
And those fancy Cakes that the patissiere makes
With names you can't even pronounce

And there's no such thing as a big beer belly
And calories don't even exist
It's all been a lie and while I don't know why
I carried on reading the list

Chocolate should be taken at least once a day
And so should a glass of red wine
Chips are so good, they're the new Super food
And Bacon for breakfast is fine

Great I thought, feeling quite hungry
Then a bell stopped my thoughts in midstream
My alarm clock had rung and my sleeping was done
It seems it was all just a dream

This dieting ain't all it's cracked up to be ...lol...xx

We Can't go back (The Boleyn Ground)

Now to all those who are blaming the new stadium
Okay let's agree to disagree
Of course it's got it's downsides on the inside and the outside
But we can't go back to where we used to be

It's true that we were happy at the Boleyn
But it's no good going on with doom and gloom
There's a block of flats that straddle
where the Bobby Moore stand stood
And the centre spot's in someone's living room

The chicken run's long gone replaced with concrete
And the Trevor Brooking stand's a park for kids
So unless we want the boys to play on swings and roundabouts
The Hammer's home is staying where it is

I know we're all frustrated that they moved us
But what we gonna do to make it right
Sit and watch the sun go down from
Barking Road or Canning Town
Or stick with it until they get it right

Now come on lads, we're Happy Hammers ain't we
Though we could all go down Green St for a laugh
And watch the game from where we used to sit back in the day
But the chances are you'd be in someone's bath

Soppy Old Sod

Now since I packed up working, I've become a soppy old sod
I can never find my glasses and my socks are usually odd
I hardly know what day it is unless it's the weekend
Or what I went upstairs for so I just come down again

I forget to pick my tablets up, when the Chemist gets them in
I found my wallet and my keys both in the biscuit tin
I sit to watch a film and pour myself a glass of red
And then I fall asleep and wake up when it's time for bed

But when I come to think of it, it's not since I retired
I always was a soppy sod, just younger and less tired
I used to think I knew stuff when I was my younger self
But it turns out I was blagging it like everybody else

So if you get to thinking that perhaps you've lost the plot
And age is finally catching up, the chances are it's not
We've always been the way we are but then it didn't show
Soppy old sod or just a bit odd ? How am I supposed to know

Strictly's Coming On

They Dance the Paso Doble as if born to swish the cape
The Matador and Bull begin, in that familiar shape
The band strike up, they start to strut,
their stuff around the floor
The story comes through, if the dance is true
and leaves you wanting more

I like the Argentine Tango, that's a favourite of mine
The deadpan face, the concentration as their legs entwine
Flying around, they own the floor, intensity abounds
You feel like you're in Argentina,
with the sights and smells and sounds

But you know of course a Viennese Waltz will mesmerise the crowd
The Fleckle and the Natural turn will hear us cheer out loud
That's all for now, I have no time, to add another one
I've got to go 'cos as you know ...
Strictly's coming on ....

Do do do do do dodo do do do do do .....

Music is Good for the Soul

Everyone loves their Music
Some say it's good for the soul
Some people go for the Classical stuff
While some people like Rock and Roll

We've all got our favourite singers
And some say that Elvis was King
Some find what they're after in the songs of Sinatra
And some like to hear Bowie sing

It's strange because they call Springsteen The Boss
And they used to say Clapton was God
But Clive Dunne took Grandad to the top of the charts
Dressed up like some soppy old sod

Now Jazz, that's a whole different ballgame
I can't seem to make that thing rhyme
It's like five different people, playing five different tunes
But all playing at the same time

There's Motown and Disco and Country
Hip Hop and Techno and Swing
Some people like the Italian Opera
Everyone's got their own thing

Whether Mozart, McCartney or Moby
Dylan or old Nat King Cole
Everyone loves their music
And it's certainly good for the soul

I've got a Mate

I've got a mate who's Muslim
And I've got a mate who ain't
But it really doesn't matter though
'cos neither one's a saint
I've got a mate who's Jewish
But we just call him Dave
I once new a dope smoking Buddhist
Who went to an early grave

I've got a friend who's German
And I've got a mate who's Greek
Thank God they both know English
Or we'd never get to speak
A couple of mates who drive Taxis
And one who worked in the docks
Some of my friends are American
And one never wears any socks

One of my friends is left handed
And one's of Jamaican descent
A bloke I once knew was about six foot two
And walked with his neck slightly bent
Quite a few of my circle are Irish
And they're always good for the craic
My neighbours came here from the Ukraine
And I don't think they want to go back

...

...

I once knew a fella with a rolled up umbrella
Who never went out in the rain
Somebody I used to work with retired
And moved out to Spain
Most of my mates now wear glasses,
We find that it helps us to see
I think Sinatra was the best singer ever
Though some of you may not agree

The point is that everyone's different
Though everyone's really the same
It's only the tags we put on them,
And sometimes the tags are to blame
I know a girl who gets her hair curled
And I must say it looks kinda quaint
I've got a mate who's Muslim
And I've got a mate who ain't

A Day at the Beach

There's sand in the back of the S U V
The cool box is full and in reach
We smell like sun lotion and salt from the ocean
Cos we're having a day at the beach

The radio's playing, old Willie is singing
A song called The time of the Preacher
The tailgate is up with my tee shirt on top
And we're watching the surf boarding teacher

The sunbeds are laying there, side by side
And the umbrella sways in the breeze
I open a beer and walk down to the pier
And paddle in up to my knees

The spray from the ocean has give me the notion
To try out a surfboard myself
But at sixty years old I think being that bold
Could only be bad for my health

So I'll sit here and lap up the sunshine
'til my skin starts to look like a peach
With a slightly pink nose and the sand 'tween my toes
We're having a day at the beach

The Review

Why do you want me to leave a review
Just 'cos I splashed out and bought something new
Are you looking for praise or a pat on the back
Or trying to make sure that I don't send it back

It seems to me you may be having misgivings
About how you do what you do for a living
How was our service ? How did we do?
Do you really like it, Did the earth move for you

Please rate the following from one up to ten
Would you go back on our website again?
Did our product meet up to your expectations
Would you recommend us to friends and relations

I ordered it, I paid for it, You sent it, I got it
I thought our transaction was buried
But it seems now we're in a relationship
I feel I should point out I'm married

Mate, it was just an adaptor
For connecting the thing to my phone
I'll remember your service 'til the end of my days
Now sod off and leave me alone ...

The Curse of Getting Older

It's the curse of getting older and the way our thoughts now run
You're still as bright as a button but the button's come undone
You've still got all your marbles but a couple fell out the bag
I gave up smoking about ten years ago
and just went to reach for a fag

Everything happened "The other day"
and most of your stories are true
You meet some old bloke down the market,
and he's five years younger than you
You know your Cholesterol numbers
but what they should be you're not sure
You know all the names of the tablets you take
but you're not certain what they're all for

You wonder what happened to football,
it used to be a man's game
You still like that girl from that programme on telly,
you just can't remember her name
You know that it's all in there somewhere,
it's just tucked away in a safe place
You think you look good when you take off your shirt,
but that probably isn't the case

You fancy a mid life crisis but the time for that's probably passed
You really should get some new glasses
but to be honest, you just can't be arsed
Maybe that's half of the problem,
'cos when everything's been said and done
It's the curse of getting older
And the way your thoughts now run

Singin' in the Rain

It's Monday and it's raining, and everyone's complaining
as they're heading out to work and getting wet
The Bus stop's by a puddle so you join the strangers huddle
and you groan because the bus ain't turned up yet

Heads are down and collars up, faces frown as folks look up
and watch around the bend for it to come
Seventeen umbrella's and that little ginger fella
who is splashing in the puddles with his mum

The ginger kid is running 'round and making patterns on the ground
he's floating lolly sticks along the gutter
He's built a little dam with the front wheel of his pram
and he laughs as water splashes on the rubber

And suddenly you realise, the truth is there before your eyes
the only way's to be a kid again
So take your time no need to dash, see a puddle, make a splash
and soon you will be Singing in the Rain

Do be do do, Do be do be do be do be....

We're still in the Running

I was born, in a nice little place, called 1954
I'd go back to that at the drop of a hat
But it just isn't there any more

Somebody took my childhood away,
Or maybe I just let it go
I just couldn't wait to get older,
But let's face it, what did I know

So I sped through the fifties and sixties,
Not paying too much attention
And ended up here and while some of it's clear,
There's a few things I thought I might mention

You don't see those national health glasses no more
With a plaster stuck over one eye
Or baggy short trousers, or back to back houses
It's all gone and I don't know why

The whistling milkman, the dog hating postman
And a bloke who delivered the coal
My nan doing washing while no one was watching
With a washboard stood over a bowl

Ha'pennys and pennies, collecting the empties,
Suet pudding and threepenny bits
Paraffin heaters and shillings in meters
And Frankie Vaughan still having hits

...

...

A quarter of Spam, three kids in one pram
And a packet of boiled sweets
Men sharpening knives and girls with beehives
And football played out in the streets

I wish I'd slowed down and just looked around
The way that I seem to do now
It's just like a race and all done at life's pace
And out of control anyhow

How did I get to be Forty years old ?
Let alone Fifty or Sixty
Three score and ten coming up 'round the bend
It's all going by way too quickly

We don't know what's coming but we're still in the running
And one thing I do know for sure
Is that I was born, in a nice little place, called 1954

Some People

Some people know me from Twitter
Some people know me from school
Some people met me on holiday
While lounging about by the pool

Some people think they might know me
But confuse me with somebody else
Some people don't want to know me
But that lot can go ... please them self

Some people send me reminders
Of me in a long ago life
Some people met me and didn't forget me
And some went to school with my wife

Some people think they remember
But somehow just can't place the face
Some won't admit how they know me
And some keep it quiet just in case

But here we all are now on Facebook
Friends and strangers and lovers
Where it's easy to see, I'm sure you'll agree
Some people are stranger than others

God Bless you all ...xx

They've Closed the Pie 'n' Mash Shop in the Roman

They ripped out the heart of the Roman
When they closed down the Pie and Mash shop
I know that they had to do running repairs
But when is this all gonna stop

I thought they'd be open by New Year
But I ain't seen no sign of it yet
I looked through the hoarding and scaffold and boarding
It don't look like there's anything left

There's still a few tiles on the wall on the right
But everything else is ripped out
The counter and doors and tables and floors
Now tell me what's that all about

Now I know we can go over Hoxton
And there's two down in Bethnal Green Road
But we need Kelly's back in the Roman
Back in the E3 postcode

I'm craving the old Two and double
When I go 'round my Mum's for the day
Hurry up Kelly's and fill up our bellies
I feel like I'm wasting away

P.S. ... They tell me they'll be open soon ...xx

Five Year Plan

I've heard people talk about five year plans
So I thought I'd get me one of those
It's nice to have some idea where you're going
And not just to follow your nose

But I don't really have much ambition
So I don't really know where to start
I'm more of a seat of the pants kind of guy
But I think I should maybe take part

Now some want to climb the corporate ladder
But for me now my working life's over
Some want to live in a faraway land
But you can't beat the white cliffs of Dover

Some want to marry the love of their lives
But I done that a long time ago
Some want to own a Ferrari
But for me, well the seats are too low

Some want to be on the Telly
While searching for fortune and fame
But I'd sooner be at home watching the Telly
I'm not very good at this game

Some want their team to win the league
While I want West Ham to survive
In five years time, I'll be sixty nine
So my plan is to still be alive

My Kitchen

The thing that I hate most about my kitchen
Is that everything is inside something else
The small bowl's in the bigger bowl
and that's inside the other bowl
And they're behind the tea cups on the shelf

My coffee mug has got a mug inside it
And the dinner plates begin a pyramid
Everything gets smaller as the stack of stuff gets taller
And the same thing happens with the saucepan lids

And while we're on the subject of the saucepans
I always seem to need the bottom one
With all this double handling
and the leaning tower dismantling
It's a wonder I get any cooking done

The sugar bowl's inside the Pyrex dishes
And the medicines are in an old toffee tin
The knives and forks and spoons
Are in a drawer without much room
And the mixing bowl has got crisps and sweeties in

The chilli sauce sits on the Piccalilli
The Tupperware fits neatly in itself
The thing that I hate most about my kitchen
Is that everything is inside something else

Or it's in the flippin' Dishwasher ...xx

The Recycling Centre

Now I've been to the Recycling centre
Or as we used to call it, the dump
I had some old bits to get rid of
And the dustmen would just get the hump

So I loaded it into the motor
And headed off down Jenkins Lane
But things didn't go quite the way that I'd planned
And you know that I'm gonna complain

Well I drove through their bit of an obstacle course
And arrived at the security hut
There was no one about so I stopped and got out
To be honest, I thought it was shut

Then a voice from somewhere said "You can't park that there"
"It's not parked, I'm just trying to get in"
He came over and looked in the back of the car
While I stood there looking at him

"What's in the box" ?, he asked me
"Rubbish" I said, being clever
"Well, I have to know what, sort of rubbish you've got
'cos we can't sling it all in together"

The electricals go in the skip over there
And old tins of paint in that cage
Old clothes and shoes and the things we can use
Get recycled, regardless of age

...

...

Now Garden waste goes into the compost
And that's round the block on the right
If it's made out of wood and it ain't any good
It'll go on the bonfire tonight

Now your General waste goes round the corner
Just sling it over the wall
So I said perhaps you can draw me a map
Just so I remember it all

Okay I said, open the gate then
He said have you got your I.D.?
It seems that they need my name and address
Oh why is this happening to me

Now what I said next can't be printed
But I'm not allowed back at the dump
I've stuck it all in to my spare Wheelie bin
And the dustman can just get the hump

New Trainers

I just bought a new pair of trainers
And I put them straight on there and then
I came out of the shop, I opened the top
And slung my old pair in the bin

Now the problem, of course, with new trainers
Is that they're so flippin' well white
Now I do look a treat with these stuck on my feet
But I'll be safe if I go out at night

Mind you they ain't quite as comfy
As the ones I just slung in the bin
But it has to be told they were about three years old
And I'm sure I'll soon wear these ones in

But for now I look like one of them old guys
That you see at the airport in June
"Grandad, you need some new trainers"
Our holiday's coming up soon

So he went out and bought them on Friday
And he's just took them out of the box
His trainers are glowing and his ankles are showing
And besides that he ain't wearing socks

Well, I guess I am one of them old guys
But I don't see myself in that way
I think of myself as a classic
Like my Reeboks that I bought today

Now I know that the Reeboks are old school
But so am I so that's alright
There's only one problem with a new pair of trainers
It's that they're so flippin' well white

Selfie Day

Today I had a selfie day
A day all to myself
No cooking, washing, ironing or shopping
Gardening or anything else

I didn't even go out in the car
I sat here in front of the telly
Eating toast and chocolate biscuits
And playing my ukelele

I had about seventeen cups of tea
And the central heating was on
I read through my newsfeed on Facebook
And recorded a Glen Campbell song

I watched an old black and white movie
But dozed off a couple of times
I ate some more chocolate biscuits
And wrote down a couple of rhymes

I know that it never stopped raining
But the truth is I just didn't care
It was warm and dry where I was inside
And I sure wasn't going out there

It's days like this that I'll remember
And I reckon it's good for your health
Today I had a selfie day
A day all to myself

Stuff

It's the stuff that we bring with us that'll prove that it was real
The photographs and object d'art are scars that never heal
It's one thing having memories but they're all in your head
It's better when you hold the things that you once held instead

That whassname that you wore round your neck
from a length of leather cord
Your Mum's old tin of buttons and your Dad's Shove Ha'penny Board
The top tier of your wedding cake from 1984
Your DVD collection that you don't watch any more

That mobile phone that you brought home that doesn't have a charger
The baccy tin with fixing in, you got from your Grandfather
A few LPs by Slade and Squeeze and one by Leo Sayer
There no chance that you'll play them again
You ain't got a record player

The bric a brac that you brought back from holidays in Spain
The hat you bought in Florida that you'll never wear again
That picture of your Mum and Dad dressed in their Sunday best
The ticket stubs you kept that night when you went out up west

It doesn't matter what it is or where you got it from
The thing is it's a part of you so bring it all along
Our memories are golden And we bring them up at will
But It's the stuff that we bring with us
That'll prove that it was real

The Moonie

We used to go to the Moonie
By the station there in Stepney Green
Most of the time we went there for swimming
But sometimes we went to get clean

Now if you don't know what the Moonie is
It's called the Municipal baths
But we come from the East End of London
And we do every thing there by halves

We used to make out it was Colditz
As they led us into the stalls
We'd plan our escape and what route we would take
In Morse code, all tapped out on the walls

"More hot water in cell number three"
We'd call to the bloke through the door
It worked like a dream as you heard next door scream
Because you were in stall number four

Then once we were all done and dusted
The bit we looked forward to most
For about "1 and 3" for a nice cup of tea
And two slices of marmalade toast

That was us done with our bathing
For at least a week if I'm being honest
It wasn't that bad 'cos at least we all had
What my mum called a Cat's lick and a promise

Sixty Three Summers

Now, I'm a man of Sixty Three Summers
And Autumns and Winters and Springs
I've been here for a while and can still raise a smile
And I've seen quite a few different things

I've been to some places and mixed with some faces
Rubbed shoulders with Rich and with Poor
With Gents and with Ladies, with good guys and baddies
Been positive and not been too sure

Of course, I've been younger and I have to say stronger
But I'd like to think never more wise
I've laughed and I've cried, but all that aside
I'm amazed still at just how time flies

Wasn't it yesterday that I turned eighteen?
Or twenty or perhaps thirty two
I can easily remember that day in September
When my old wedding ring was new

I'm sure it's no more than a couple of years
Since my Son took his first breath of air
But now he's a Grandad and I know that ain't too bad
But how did that time disappear

...

...

As Frank said, Regrets ?, I've had a few
But to quote him again, well That's Life
You can't make an omelette without breaking some eggs
And I've broken some ... Ask my wife

It's not over though, I've a long way to go
And I'm sure that I'll make a few blunders
But the problem I'm having and it's a little bit nagging
Is what happened to those Sixty Three Summers??

Another day in Paradise

There's a line of boats out there on the horizon
As the sun comes up and lights the morning sky
The waves wash last night's footprints
from the beach along the shore
And a lit up cruise ship sails serenely by

The gulls fly in formation as they skim the ocean waves
The sandpipers stand still and face the breeze
An early morning fisherman casts his line into the surf
With his trousers rolled up just below his knees

People out on bicycles, riding side by side
Lovers strolling slowly hand in hand
A lady with a ziploc bag, collecting shells and with a rag
Carefully cleans off the grains of sand

The deckchair sellers set the chairs to face the morning sun
And no one really cares about the price
The coffee's brewed and tasting good
and everything looks like it should
And so begins another lovely day in paradise

For Robyn

She used to come to Grandad's for the weekend
We used to go to Pizza hut for tea
We'd sit and watch the Disney films on telly
And she'd drop off to sleep on my settee

I'd carry her upstairs into her bedroom
And watch her as she snuggled in her bed
I'd smile when I remembered all the things we'd done that day
And laugh when I remembered things she'd said

I miss my baby girl now she's a grown up
But love her just the same as way back when
She may now be a mum of two
But still my "Missy Dumplings" too
And I still get to hug her now and then

The years go by so quickly we don't notice
And the future soon becomes the distant past
Our special bond is still as strong and family goes on and on
Thank heaven that some things are built to last

Oh to be in England

Country lanes and summer rains
Custard Creams and daisy chains
Castles, streams and coastal trains
And marmalade on toast

Stately homes and garden gnomes
Candy floss and Ice cream cones
Seaside piers and Shakespeare's bones
And a lovely Sunday roast

Cricket on the village green
Crumpets, tea and Heinz baked beans
Thatched roofs and God save the Queen
And day trips to the coast

Country walks and Cheddar gorge
Bobby Moore and the blacksmith's forge
Saucy postcards and the cross of St. George
Oh to be in England ...

I Don't Understand

There's quite a few things that I don't understand
And a few that I can't put to rest
Like why are they still showing Birds of a Feather
And who the hell is Kanye West

Algebra, German and Towie
And children who scream all the time
Matt finished cars and Reality stars
And kids who don't like chocolate limes

The meaning of life has escaped me
Unless Monty Python were right
People who don't like what I like
And why all my clothes are so tight

Whatever happened to Soap on a Rope
You never see that any more
Why do I now quite like Marzipan icing
When I never liked it before

What is Victoria's secret
And why did they end The Fast Show
And what is the story with that bloke on Corrie
No scratch that I don't want to know

There's quite a few things that I don't understand
Like the point of a three legged stool
And I don't even know what a Logarithm is
But I'm sure they taught that one at school

I Fancy Pie and Mash Today

I fancy Pie and Mash today
But I really don't know where to go
Barking Road or Bethnal Green
Or Chrisp St. I don't know

There's Hoxton or Broadway Market
But I ain't going south of the Thames
I got seasick once on the Woolwich Ferry
And I ain't going through that again

Now I know that there's one up in Lakeside
And one over Leytonstone too
But Kelly's ain't open down Roman Road yet
So I don't really know what to do

There's Robins there in Wanstead High St
But the Beckton one didn't survive
I've heard there's a good one in Clacton
But the wife doesn't fancy the drive

I fancy the old two and double
And the Mrs. says she'll have the same
Liquor, White pepper and Vinegar
You know it's all part of the game

A fork and a spoon and some orange squash
The accessories for those in the know
I fancy Pie and Mash today
But I really don't know where to go

There's a Waiter Here ...

There's a waiter here walking round singing
He must have come in the wrong door
We've been coming here, for year upon year
And not known this happen before

They're usually a downright miserable bunch
Buenos Dias is rarely heard said
And don't even try to catch one of them's eye
You'll just see the back of his head

When night comes around and you're sat in the lounge,
Killing time and watching the dancers
Don't even think about ordering a drink
They'll be too busy picking up the glasses

But the fact that they're so antisocial
Saves me a fortune on tips
It's chicken and egg and you give what you get
I leave them my old Olive pips

But as we're going home today
I don't suppose we'll know for sure
Just why he's walking around singing
And if he came in the wrong door

The Tap

I had a couple of mates come 'round
To fix our leaking tap
It only needed a washer
And these two would soon deal with that

The bloke in the shop said "You can't fix these ones,
They don't have a washer as such"
So I pick out a new one, a Chrome, Red and Blue one,
And then the bloke told me how much

So anyway, after a glass of water
From a tap that cost much more than mine,
I pay and we leave but I truly believe,
The dripping one would have been fine

But the guys do the job, for a couple of bob
And I fill up the sink when they're gone
I'm not being funny, but for that kind of money,
It should turn it's flippin' self on

Well anyway that was yesterday
And now it's a whole brand new day
I've got nothing else to complain about
So now I'll just be on my way

I have stuff to do and I know you do too
But as usual I'll still be around
Just hold on though, before we all go,
What is that strange dripping sound ?...

Toothpaste

Now when it comes to toothpaste I use Colgate
Always have and probably always will
The trouble is they make so many different ones these days
It's hard to work out which one fits the bill

So, do I need the Cavity Protection?
Total Whitening or maybe Pro Relief
Or something that they called advanced,
Or maybe I should take a chance
On one that repairs the Enamel on your teeth

The Max Fresh or perhaps the Expert Softmint
The Deep clean whitening or flippin' Sensifoam
Sensitive or 2 in 1 ? I'll never get my shopping done
I'm confused now and I can't be on my own

I'm looking for the one that just say's Colgate
The way it used to do back in the day
'cos if the one I get is wrong and the minty taste's a bit too strong
There's no chance I can throw the tube away

So I'm scanning all the toothpaste shelves in Asda
I don't need these decisions in my life
I think that I might get the one with the stripes in
And next time leave the choice up to the wife

Trying to Book a Holiday

Now I was having a look 'cos I wanted to book
A week in July in the sun
But I had to look twice when I noticed the price
And thought they were having me on

I thought, Flippin' hell when I checked the hotel,
And that's not including the flights
So I had a quick thought and I thought that we ought
To cut it to maybe five nights

Then I looked at B A for what they had to say
But they couldn't help so instead
I checked Ryanair and with Easy Jet there,
Both flying out of Stansted

Well I checked on the fares, it was like buying shares
I don't want to purchase the plane
So I looked on Jet2 and Thomas Cook too
And they both come out 'bout the same

Now there's nothing conclusive about all inclusive
But sometimes full board can be nice
But I'm thinking half board is all we can afford
And I'm not sure of that at this price

So perhaps B&B or an afternoon tea
Or a caravan down at Southend
But I know that won't do so what else can I do
But to juggle the numbers again

...

With my spirits now sinking I sat here then thinking
perhaps a long weekend away
It was all a bit scary so I thought I'd ring Mary
and find out what she had to say

She agreed it was clear it was all very dear
but she did sound a little half hearted
Then she said "Yeah I know, but I still want to go"
so here I am back where I started

It's a tough life ... lol ...xx

A Man of a Certain Age

Now I'm a man of a certain age
But I'm not certain what that age is
I thought that it ran chronologically
And you just added up all the years

But now fifty is the new forty
And staying in is the new going out
That's a twenty percent reduction in age
And ten years you've forgotten about

Now twenty percent off when you're twenty years old
Means that you've just turned sixteen
But nobody wants to be younger at twenty
That's when you're living life's dream

It's when you get older and look over your shoulder
And you'd like to get some of them back
But Friday is now the new Saturday
And Orange is the new black

Now I was born in the year of our lord
Nineteen hundred and fifty and four
And I can't work out what is twenty percent
So I'm doing my sums to be sure

So we'll start with your street door number
Add eighteen and take away ten
Take out the number you very first thought of
And halve what you're left with and then

Add in the year England won the World cup
Take out Disney's dwarves and you'll see
I'm sure that's much better than twenty percent
Oh Bugger ... I'm still Sixty three

Remember When we would Go Out at Eleven

Remember when we would go out at eleven?
These days we're in our pyjamas by seven
We used to drink Whiskey and Vodka and Gin
But now it's more Tea, with a Biscuit dipped in

The music was loud and Disco was king
We'd stay out all night and we'd do our own thing
But now our own thing doesn't work out that way
We've had a result if we can stay out all day

We walk past the night clubs with queues at the door
We know that we've probably been in there before
But the chances are then it was called something else
And we laugh at the kids though we did it ourself

Night after night we'd go out without thinking
Doing what people today call Binge drinking
To us it was just going out for a beer
But these days I'd much sooner be sitting here

We smoked all our cigarettes when we were young
But of course, now we know it's not good for your lungs
The cocktails we drunk that would give us the shivers
But these days we're told we must think of our livers

I'm glad that we did it, the time of our lives
But time passed and we became Husbands and Wives
Remember when we would go out at eleven?
These days we're in our pyjamas by seven

Ode to a Cinnamon Swirl

Now I know I'm a bit of a fat bloke
And I may seem a little obsessed
With chocolate and cakes and biscuits and sweeties
And pastries and pies and the rest

But we went into Starbucks on Sunday
Just Mary and me and the girls
Amongst all the cakes and the muffins and bakes
I spotted their cinnamon swirls

Now, we ain't been in Starbucks for ages
It's Costa for us as you know
But a new one has opened up just 'round the corner
And we thought that we'd give it a go

Anyway back to the dainties
And back to the cinnamon swirls
The lovely soft icing and squishy sultanas
And the way that it kind of untwirls

The way that your fingers get sticky
Thank God that they give you a knife
You can cut off the bit without much icing
And offer that bit to the wife

You can keep all your poppy seed muffins
And your shortbread with chocolate and toffee
I don't want a biscuit and I'm not gonna risk it
When I'm having a nice cup of coffee

Now I know I'm a bit of a fat bloke
And I may seem a little obsessed
But a cinnamon swirl out of Starbucks
Puts everything else to the test

Our Great Grandkids will Read This One Day (Facebook)

Now, we're charting our own social history
Our Great Grandkids will read this one day
They'll learn all our innermost secrets
And learn how we work rest and play

They won't have to traipse through old archives
Or sit in a library for ages
They'll just turn on some new electronic device
And pull up our old Facebook pages

They'll know what we had for our breakfast
And what time we all said goodnight
They'll know how you voted in Brexit
And what kind of music we liked

They'll read about hospital visits
And nights on the town with our mates
They'll soon know the truth about us in our youth
School-days school friends and first dates

Well let's give them something to look at
But maintain a wee bit of mystery
Let's not embarrass the hell out of them
When they're checking their family history

So leave your dirty washing in the basket
And your fashion faux pa's tucked away
Keep your own council and avoid all the scandal
Our Great Grandkids will read this one day

Where does the Time Go ?

The years go by quicker now, as we get older
A fact that you just can't deny
A year when you're ten is a lifetime and then
When you're sixty just watch it fly by

Six months have gone now since Christmas
But we only just took down the tree
And the kids now say Grandad, that's ages away
Just wait 'til you're older, you'll see

Fifty Two years since we won the World Cup
And I remember that only too well
Thirty Six years since Abba split up
And that seems like last year as well

Thirty Four years since we married
The blink of an eye at first glance
Thirty Eight years since John Lennon died
And still no one gives peace a chance

Nine years since I've given up smoking
But still sometimes reach for my fags
Three years since Asda and Sainsbury's
Started charging for carrier bags

Grandchildren now having kids of their own
And more and more wrinkles on show
Forty three years since Starsky and Hutch
Tell me, Where does the Time Go ? ...

Me and Les

I've been out today to the driving range
With my old mate Les and our clubs
But back in the day, that wasn't the way
We used to meet then in the pubs

Les's hair was much darker then
And mine was somewhat thicker
Both of our waistlines were considerably smaller
And we both moved a little bit quicker

We swung at some balls and we swore at them all
And then we both went for a coffee
His shoulder was aching and my leg was hurting
And we left our clubs out in the lobby

It was good to catch up, sat there over a cup
And we chatted as we always do
Putting the world right, and having a quick bite
A recipe both tried and true

Well anyway we went our separate ways
He said that he couldn't be late
A great day indeed so let's follow the lead
Same time and place next week mate ? ...

A Cold Day in London

Now there's snow down in Bow and in Beckton
And all over London today
It's coming and going, first sunny then snowing
And it's probably heading your way

It's freezing in Ealing and Ilford
And some of the schools have been closed
Trains have been cancelled and schedules been scrambled
So a day off will go unopposed

Now Wimbledon Common is covered in snow
The Beast from the East has arrived
While it looks very nice, all twinkling with ice
I do hope that the Wombles survived

Now they've got some in Tottenham they tell me
And it's falling again in East Ham
Vicky park's covered but there's food in the cupboard
So I'm staying right here where I am

Don't go out today 'less you have to
But keep warm and dry anyway
There's snow down in Bow and in Beckton
And all over London today

Jacuzzi

I've just had a Jacuzzi, cos I thought it would amuse me,
to feel those bubbles tickling my bum
And you know that I was right,
I could have stayed in there all night,
or at least I'd wait for dinner time to come

But we're going out tonight, and Mary thought it wasn't right,
to go out in my still wet swimming shorts
So I've come upstairs to change,
because she's right, it would be strange,
and I've put on that new tee shirt that I bought

We're going into Malaga, so I thought that
I would challenge her,
to be showered and have her hair done in an hour
Of course she said she would,
but I never thought she could,
and I don't think it will happen anyhow

So we're gonna catch the train, into the city once again,
to shop and eat and drink with time to spare
And although we're there to party,
I'll still get my Skinny Latte,
Cos I know that there's a Costa Coffee there..

London Underground

There's a girl sitting next to me knitting
And a little boy picking his nose
A bloke wearing red bluetooth headphones
And I think that he's playing Morse code

Dit daDit Dit Dit is all I can hear
And it's starting to get on my nerves
And the kid who was picking has now started kicking
And he'll soon get what he deserves

Somebody just said hello to a stranger
In a voice just a little too loud
Everyone else rolled their eyes and tutted
Don't he know that's not allowed?

There's a lady with two bags of shopping
So I get up and give her my seat
She opens her bag and takes out a rag
And wipes something off of her feet

A girl just got on with a buggy
So I helped her, the way that you do
But when I looked in to smile at the baby
She was wheeling a little Shih tzu

The train lurches out of the station
And everyone slides to the right
A bloke and his wife hold on for dear life
They look like they've been out all night

Someone is eating a burger and chips
The sights and the smells and the sounds
London really comes into its own
Whenever it goes ... Underground

Spring Cleaning in Autumn

I hope that the season police don't find out
But I've spent all the morning Spring cleaning
The net curtains are all in the washing machine
And the bathroom is positively gleaming

The Dyson has been working overtime
I even swept under the bed
The washing is done and hung out in the sun
But I should be out there instead

I got out the new feather dusters
I do like their soft springy feeling
I flicked all the corners and pictures and mirrors
And the light that hangs down from the ceiling

The windows are smelling of Windolene
And the cushions all smell of Febreze
But mixed with the smell of the bleach and Lenor
Hold on, I'm going to sneeze

Now here's the thing, I know it's not Spring
But it is such a lovely bright day
Do you think I should tell 'em I Spring clean in Autumn ?
Oh sod it, It's done anyway

I've got too Many Tee Shirts

Now, I'm told I've got too many tee shirts
And some of them may have to go
So I'm having a bit of a clear out
And thought that you might like to know

It seems that we've run out of space for them all
And the time to be brutal has come
So I'm getting them out of the drawers and wardrobes
And sorting them out one by one

Well the first ones I see are the Beatles shirts
So that's five that are going nowhere
A couple of new ones and one or two blue ones
And a green one that I regularly wear

Now the Disney ones all carry memories
As do the two from New York
And the one from Hong Kong, I ain't had that one long
And if only this baby could talk

There's the two that I took from the covers of my books
And three different ones say Old Guys Rule
Well we know that that's true, so what can I do
To throw them away would be cruel

The West Ham shirts ain't really tee shirts
So obviously they stay where they are
And I still can't let go of the one from Orlando
My favourite tee shirt by far

...

...

There is an old white one and then there's that tight one
And those two can go for a start
But as for the others ?...Tee shirts are like lovers
And should be kept close to your heart

So the rest can go back where they came from
But you can't say that I didn't try
And I'm going down Roman Road market today
There's a tee shirt I wanted to buy

I'm Not a Tottenham Supporter

When I was at school, I went out with a girl
Whose dad was a hospital porter
A nice enough bloke but now here's the joke
He was only a Tottenham supporter

Now you get in a mess when you try to impress
So when he assumed I was one too
I decided to just let it go for a while
Well what else can a lovestruck boy do

We got on alright, then one Friday night
He asked me to go to the game
Spurs were playing West Ham the next day
Down at the old White Hart Lane

Now she thought that this was a great idea
And asked if she could come too
I did have to laugh when she offered her scarf
Which was White and a strange Navy Blue

So I stood with the Spuds in the North stand
And cheered as the teams were brought on
They got their reward when old Gilzean scored
But their cheering went on for too long

Now Greavsie had moved from Spurs to West Ham
So cheering for him was alright
But not, it would seem when he scored for our team
And that nearly started a fight

So that was me sussed as an Hammer
And the journey home was a bit raw
I never saw him or his daughter again
But we did come away with a draw

The Senses of Lakeside

Ah, the smell of plastic coming from the shoe shop
As I walk along the ground floor in Lakeside
Mixes with the smell of Krispy Donuts
And makes me feel all whassname, deep inside

Then Lush and Rush and Thorntons and the Wimpy
All adding to the aromatic score
Then a hundred different ringtones
from a hundred different iPhones
Assault my ears outside the Disney store

So into Marks and Spencer's to relieve and ease my senses
But of course I have to pass the Fragrance shop
Up the escalator, out the door and see you later
Then L'Occitane will catch me on the hop

I smell the coffee coming out of Starbucks
And I'm blinded by the bling from Beaverbrooks
Then I felt a little weakness just outside Victoria's secret
So I thought it best I didn't take a look

Up one more flight and now we're in the food hall
With sights and smells that made my heart beat quicker
And then the smell that led me on,
the one that showed me right from wrong
I love the smell of Pie and Mash and Liquor

Autumn

The sky has turned a leaden grey
The Sun has run for cover
The leaves are falling from the trees
The summer's truly over

The days are getting shorter
The nights are drawing in
The heat has left the evening air
The colder nights begin

Autumn smiles that certain smile
Her time has come again
Lights turned on and curtains drawn
Against the wind and rain

The temperatures are dropping
And it feels a little strange
Just turn the central heating up
And celebrate the change ...xx

We're Home

Things that I'm looking forward to
Now that the holiday is done
A nice cup of tea and a biscuit
And going to see my old Mum

Ringing my son on the telephone
To see how the world's been with him
"Glad you're home Dad", I can hear him say now,
And to see how the Grandkids have been

Sitting in front of the telly ..
Driving on the right side of the road
Driving on the right side of the Car for that matter
And cooking a nice Sausage toad

Shopping at Asda, walking 'round London
And sleeping in my own bed
Going for coffee and driving past Starbucks
And going to Costa instead

Having the little ones come next weekend
To stay with Nanny and Grandad
McDonald's on Friday, movie night Saturday
Being back home's not so bad

Well here we are then, be it ever so humble
Where the heart is and where I belong
I have no idea when we'll next go away ...
But you can bet that it won't be too long

I Like a Cup of Tea

I like a cup of Tea to go with breakfast
And I love a cup of Coffee later on
And when it comes to evening time,
I like a glass of full Red wine
And another one of those when that one's gone

I like the Fruit and Fibre for my breakfast
And a Bacon Roll for lunch can be quite nice
And when it comes to dinner,
I find Salmon is a winner
Or Chicken Curry on a bed of rice

I like a slice of toast at night with jam on
And a Chocolate Hob nob 'fore I go to bed
Dipped into some Ice cold milk
that then goes down as smooth as silk
Or perhaps a Jaffa cake or two instead

I like to snack on crisps and chocolate raisins
And Cadbury's Fruit and Nut makes my heart sing
I'm going down to Asda for my shopping in a minute
I wonder what delights today will bring ?

It's the little things ain't it ?

Christmas Shopping

The Brussells sprouts haven't been picked yet
The King Edward's are still in the ground
The Pickles are still in their jars on the shelves
And the Turkeys are still running round

It's only one week until Christmas
Just seven days 'til the big day
They'd best get a move on and get themselves sorted
'cos we're going out there today

We're doing the Christmas food shopping
You'd think the world was going to end
Two shopping trolleys as we walk around Asda
Lord knows how much money we'll spend

But I'm not complaining, I love it
The house will be full of good stuff
The problem is so will my belly
And I think that bad boy's had enough

So don't overdo it like last year
You know that you all bought too much
Alright get your sweeties and biscuits and dainties
But shop with a much lighter touch.

But if you could stay home until lunchtime
And give us free run on the shelves
I'll give you a shout once we've been sorted out
And then you can go help yourselves ...xx

Christmas is Coming

Well, that's the shopping finished
and the presents are all wrapped
The Turkey's in the freezer
and the table plan is mapped
There's wine and beer to help good cheer
and soft drinks for the kids
There's crisps and sweets and nuts and treats,
on plates like dustbin lids

The Christmas lights are twinkling
and the cards have all been read
The tree is decked with balls and snow
with an angel overhead
The Holly wreath with berries,
hanging on the red street door
It's more than looking, a bit like Christmas,
it's nearly here for sure

There's still the odd thing left to do,
just as there always is
Two full days left, time enough,
to get into a tizz
Whatever happens, between now and then,
One thing will always be clear
Turkey and tinsel, food by the skinful,
I Love this time of the year ...

Christmas Eve

It started on a night like this, two thousand years now gone
In the dark and Midnight sky, a brand new bright star shone
Those who saw it followed it, for they knew where it lead
To Bethlehem, a manger where a baby lay his head

An infant child was born to us to take away our sins
The weight of the world placed on his shoulders
The light of the world within
It's Christmas eve we celebrate the birth of our salvation
Let's not forget the reason for this season's incarnation

I believe, if we believe we'll find the peace inside
And love of life will follow when we get ourselves onside
The child became man and sacrificed, ev'rything for you
Be nice to people in his name it's the least that you can do

Merry Christmas

Christmas Past

I remember Christmas morning as a nipper
We'd get up bright and early, as you do
We'd have a lot of fun and "Accidentally" wake our mum
And probably wake the next door neighbours too

We'd get two shiny pennies in our stocking
A pair of socks in case our feet got cold
A bag of Chocolate Money,
and some chews that tasted funny
And a little canvas bag of Spanish Gold

A spud gun, and a pack of Liquorice Allsorts
Some marbles and a box of coloured chalk
A Yoyo that lit up and a Mickey Mouse Egg Cup
Or a little plastic Robot that could talk

A compass and a ball or a Mouth Organ
A Dalek or a metal spinning top
The latest Beano annual and a wooden football rattle
And a laughing bag that sometimes wouldn't stop

We'd make the paper chains for decoration
And cut up last year's cards with pinking shears
We'd use them then, for tags on peoples presents
Recycling 101, the early years

All the fun we had back then, we'd love to do it all again
And if you really wanted to you could
But I'd like to see you give your kids,
a tangerine like our Mum's did
Or a glider that was made of balsa wood

Boxing Day

Who got a new scarf for Christmas
Who else got new pants and socks
Who got some sweets and some chocolate treats
Wrapped up in a Chrismassy box

Who got a new pair of slippers
Who got Chanel Number 5
Who got some bling or electronic thing
What a time to be alive

So now we're all counting our blessings
And our gifts have all been put away
With Christmas day now done and dusted
We're chilling out on Boxing Day

I hope we're all keeping the spirit
Of peace and goodwill to all men
Be of good cheer and maybe next year
Santa will come back again

God Bless us everyone ...xx

Friends

We talk about and celebrate, all our yesterdays
And together we look forward to tomorrow
We share our triumphs and disasters,
and our happy ever afters
Along with all our joys and sometimes sorrow

We revel in the memories of our lives in yesteryear
And laugh at pictures of us in our youth
We poke each other in the ribs
and sometimes tell each other fibs
And somewhere in the banter find the truth

We ask each other questions like, do you remember when
And whatsisname the bloke who lived next door
We reminisce on happy times
and sometimes read between the lines
But then we all know, that's what friends are for

Farewell to the Fields

The fields of Athenry lie low,
as if they know it's time to go
and once again we leave this place we love
It doesn't matter where we roam
I never mind the going home
but this time I may need a little shove

A weekend isn't long enough
to spend with people that you love,
but we'll be back again before too long
The countryside and cities
and the anecdotes and ditties
could inspire anyone to write a song

But writing songs ain't what I do,
I just write verse like this for you
and hope I can portray the time we've had
A day of mixed emotions,
and of new ideas and notions
and happiness mixed with a little sad

And now to face the flight again,
propellers, bumps and shakes and rain
we head for London City and our home
We drive away and turn and smile
and bid farewell to the Emerald Isle
and the fields of Athenry we've loved and known

I Can Still

I can still smell the Vosene medicated shampoo
I can still feel it stinging my eyes
I can still hear the sound as the twin tub went round
I can still taste my Nan's Apple Pies

I can still see the posters on my bedroom wall
That covered the little damp patches
I can still hear the records played on the Dansette
You somehow got used to the scratches

I can still see that black and white telly
In the corner of my Nan's front room
And how we all gathered around it and watched
As Neil Armstrong walked on the moon

I can still taste the pink semolina
That they served up for afters at school
I can still hear my teacher hollering out
Ross, stop acting the fool

But of course this is all in the past now
Though I'm certain you won't be surprised
I can still smell the Vosene medicated shampoo
And I can still feel it stinging my eyes

Remembrance Day

We stand in silence heads hung low
and watch as they march past
Old Men, Young Men, Wives and Children,
ev'ry creed and cast
Remembering the fallen
who we sent away to war
Proud of them and what they did
and what they did it for

The rights and wrongs of war itself
are there for all to see
They ultimately gave their lives
for our democracy
Salute them for the sacrifice
they made without regret
They will have all been lost in vain
if ever we forget

I was Born in 1954

I was born in 1954 and look, I'm still alive
I used to drink water straight from the tap
The Lord knows how I survived

I went out without a mobile phone
And didn't come home 'til dark
I played in the street in the winter
And in summer went over the park

I got in the bath every Friday,
When my mum dragged it in from the yard
I walked to school every morning
And never thought that was too hard

We only had two telly channels
And they were both in black and white
And the highlight was watching The London Palladium,
At 8'O'clock on Sunday night

The nearest I got to an iPad
Was one time when I got a sty
And of course I wore National Health Glasses
On account of my lazy left eye

My Nan lived upstairs in our house
And the toilet was out in the back
We used to pick up empty lemonade bottles
And get tuppence when we took them back

...

...

We went to Canvey Island for our holidays
And stayed on a Caravan site
Again with the outside toilet
We hated that walk late at night

We set off all our own fireworks
And in Winter we made our own sleds
We learned all life's lessons and counted our blessings
When Mum tucked us into our beds

But above all of this we were happy
'specially when Mum learned to drive
I was born in 1954 and look, I'm still alive

Second Hand

When I moved out of my Mum's place
That was when my Nan moved in
And she gave us some of her second hand stuff
So our new life could begin

She gave us her old kitchen table
Of course with the four matching chairs
A glass bowl for stuff and if that weren't enough
A wardrobe that she kept upstairs

My mate's Dad was selling his cooker
So I bought that from him for a fiver
Mary's mum gave us her spare chest of drawers
'cos we didn't have one of them either

My Auntie had give us a canteen of cutlery
That she'd got in a charity raffle
And the mat on the floor as you came through the door
Came off of a stall in Whitechapel

Our first fridge had come from a friend of my mum
And the telly, we bought second hand
And soon we had all that we needed
And we moved in together as planned

We did go and buy a new washing machine
And that made our kitchen complete
My mum went and bought some new furniture
So we had her old three piece suite

But now that won't do, they want everything new
And getting in debt is a charm
We started off with second hand stuff
And it didn't do us any harm

I Wish we had Snow like the Old Days

Oh, I wish we had snow like the old days
When we measured in inches and feet
And it looked liked cake icing, on top of the dustbins
Outside everyone's house in your street

Icicles hung from the gutters
Like tear drops suspended in space
The world looked so wonderful dressed up in white
And spider's webs looked like white lace

Winter was a true time of wonder
Made special when covered in snow
And at night with the street lights, of sodium yellow
It took on a strange eerie glow

Snowmen and snowballs and mittens and hats
Small yellow patches that were left by the cats
Snow angels made on the ground in the park
Staying and playing 'til well after dark

I'm sure time has clouded my memories
But they stay now forever as sweet
Oh, I wish we had snow like the old days
When we measured in inches and feet

Sinatra Sings

It's twenty years since Frank passed on
But we still have all his classic songs
I'll list some now but where to start?
New York New York or Young at Heart

The Tender trap, Come fly with me
As time goes by and Didn't We
Songs we loved and songs we'd sing
Like the classic, I've got the world on a string

Nice 'n Easy, It was a very good year
All those songs we love to hear
Songs I still sing for my wife
Like All the way and of course That's Life

Something Stupid and Leroy Brown
The unmistakable Sinatra sound
Singing I get a kick out of you
And humming Do be do be do

I'm sure I've missed some favourites
And I'm sure you thought I might
But never Loves been good to me
Or Strangers in the night

Fly me to the moon you sang
And gave us Night and day
God bless and thank you Blue eyes
For doing it your Way

The Neighbour

I once had a neighbour who borrowed stuff
But never brought anything back
A screwdriver here and a Monkey wrench there
And once an old hydraulic jack

A Stapler, a Clothes horse, my spare secateurs
And a socket set extension bar
And he once took the plunge for a bucket and sponge
When he wanted to clean his car

Nothing of any real value at all
And to be fair, I never asked for them back
But it was almost as if, he thought they were his
And forgot about any comeback

One day I saw him walk up my drive
So I thought that this time I'd be clever
He asked if I had a spare mobile charger
And I lied and I told him I never

Then when he was having a barbeque
He borrowed my four fold up chairs
The ones that we take to the beach in the car
And that created a state of affairs

The Mrs said that I should ask for them back
And that morning he knocked on my door
He said that he needed to borrow a suitcase
But didn't say what the hell for

He seemed to be in quite a hurry
So I thought I'd wait 'til the next day
In the morning I found what the suitcase was for
When the removal van was pulling away

He's buggered off with all my stuff ...

Shaving

I cut myself shaving on Sunday
Now some of you may find this strange
But if you'd like to sit down and listen
I'll do all I can to explain

When a man gets to a certain age
Hairs start to grow in strange places
I don't mean, you know, whassname and that
But in and around on our faces

I noticed a couple of rogue grey hairs
Right here on the top of my ear
It's something that ladies might not understand
But something us old fellas fear

While I try to keep well groomed and tidy
My eyesight ain't quite what it was
So I go at the ears with a razor
Once I've taken my glasses off

Now I'm taking a couple of tablets
With the purpose of thinning my blood
So the tiniest nick and it started to drip
And soon ended up as a flood

Well It looked like a scene out of Psycho
As the blood swirled around in the shower
Or Custer's last stand that had got out of hand
And it went on for over an hour

....

...

I tried all that caper with toilet paper
And then with some pink Cotton Wool
But the blood kept on coming, first dripping then running
I weren't getting nowhere at all

But Mary then came to the rescue
With a Styptic stick stopping the flow
I think I'll just go to the Barber in future
And leave it to those in the know

Wendy Henderson

Her name was Wendy Henderson
She came from Bethnal Green
She lived with her mother, her sister and brother
when she left home to follow her dream

She wanted to be an actress
And the West End was where she was bound
So off she strode along Cambridge Heath Road
And into the underground

Her nickname was once Bendy Wendy
And her dancing they said was the worst
They'd see when she turned up on Strictly
But she had to become famous first

So with stars in her eyes, a head full of dreams
And to be honest, not much of a plan
She went off to seek fame and fortune
With her Oyster card held in her hand

She'd seen all the stars on the telly
And she wanted to be one of those
She got off the train at Chancery Lane
And walked through to Charing Cross Road

She walked past the old Palace Theatre,
There was some Harry Potter thing on
And turned into Shaftesbury Avenue
Knowing this wouldn't take long

...

...

Someone was bound to spot her,
As she strolled past The Queens and Les Mis
Then past The Guilgud and still feeling quite good
She loved the idea of showbiz

She'd not heard of the show at the old Apollo
It was Cat on a Hot tin Roof
She went for a nose but the doors were all closed,
It was too early to tell you the truth

So she went in Mcdonalds for breakfast and
By this stage began to despair
And before she knew where she was going
She ended up in Leicester Square

As it started to rain she got back on the train
And straight back towards Bethnal Green
She knew that she'd be in showbiz one day
But perhaps wait 'til she turned thirteen

West Ham United

Halfway down the Barking Road, heading east from Canning Town
There was a little patch of grass, that we called hallowed ground
A field of dreams or so it seems to any West Ham fan
And anyone who, donned the claret and blue,
Was lauded from the stands

Always known as Happy Hammers, win or lose or draw
We're always in there, with a shout, you couldn't ask for more
We'll lose to the smallest, struggling teams
And then beat the biggest of sides
Then when it comes, to the matches that matter,
The bridesmaid and never the bride

Our heroes go back in the annals of football,
From the skills of the great Bobby Moore
To the game where Di Canio, caught that cross,
'cos their goalkeeper lay on the floor
Trevor Brooking, Martin Peters, and the goalscoring hero Geoff Hurst
We all love to watch England winning a game
But West Ham United come first

So whether you're a Chelsea fan, a Gooner or a Spud
I'm sure your team inspires you and really pumps your blood
But I come from the East End of London
And that's what made me who I am
I'm sure there must be other teams,
But there's only one West Ham

Old Jokes

I got up a bit later this morning,
I usually get up around dawn
But Dawn doesn't mind, she's the real friendly kind
And the curtains are usually drawn

Now that joke's so old it's got whiskers
But then, truth be told, so have I
And the old ones are sometimes the best ones
But that doesn't always apply

They say that a good wine gets better
But our eyesight and memory get worse
The old songs are better than the ones they sing now
But with jokes it can be the reverse

Four different fonts walked in to my bar
But we don't serve that type in here
Money can't buy you happiness
But then again it can buy you beer

An old song is there for the singing
And a good joke deserves to be told
But don't tell the one about "My wife's going on holiday"...
That one is really too old

No Heating

I've got no hot water or heating
There's Brass Monkeys and welders for hire
I long for the day's you came in from the cold
And just threw some coal onto the fire

At least then you knew how to fix it
And it didn't cost you the earth
"It's Eighty six pounds for the first half hour Sir"
And then they see how much you're worth

But I guess I should just bite the bullet
And call British Gas round today
I must call my boss, about a day off
And see just what she has to say

But anyway, I'm sure there's a bright Side
And I'm gonna search high and low
Oh yeah, I just had a nice cup of tea
And I don't think that it's gonna snow

So onwards and upwards, or under the duvet
At least 'til the Heating Man knocks
Keep yourselves Dry, Or at least you can try
Goodbye ... Now, where are my Thermal Socks? ....

Essentials

The tea caddy's almost on empty
And the milk in the fridge has run out
The biscuit tin feels as light as a feather
Which all leaves me now in no doubt

I'll have to pop up to the grocery shop
'cos the essentials, they are ... well, essential
The truth is you see, that without my tea
I can be a touch ... temperamental

Now when I say the caddy's near empty
There's probably eight tea bags left
And maybe a quarter of a pint of milk
But what if I should have a guest?

So I'll just shoot upstairs and get ready
Well, of course after I've drunk my tea
I think I'll just risk it and have one more biscuit
And it's then up to Asda for me

Anyone need anything ? ...

Halloween

Tonight is the night of All Hallows
When Ghoulies and Ghosties abound
The night we make sure that our homes are secure
'cos we know something evil's around

Witches fly by on their broomsticks
There's a cold haunted chill in the air
Monsters and Zombies again roam the Earth
And the living must take extra care

The children go out Trick or Treating
There's a skeleton hung from the door
Skulls and Black Cats and Cobwebs and Bats
And things that the undead adore

Pumpkins that glow in the windows
And noises from places unseen
So lock all your doors, just to be sure
For tonight is, again, HALLOWEEN

Barbara Windsor

Gawd Bless ya Barbara Windsor, we'll all miss ya
Although we know you ain't gone nowhere yet
That wicked old disease that now afflicts ya
Is gonna take you from us, bit by bit

From "Carry On" to Peggy in "Eastenders"
A National treasure we claim as our own
From Shoreditch church to "Chitty Chitty Bang Bang"
From "Twang" to "Entertaining Mr Sloane"

Whether playing Marie Lloyd or Saucy Nancy
That twinkle and that laugh were always there
"Fings ain't what they used to be" now Barbara
But I want to let you know that we all care

A Dame Commander of the British Empire
I think you'll find them Sparra's singing now
Gawd Bless ya Barbara Windsor we'll all miss ya
But I'm gonna watch a Carry On film now

The Old Gits Club

We meet every Tuesday in Costa
We're known as the Old Gits Club
Just three older fellas who once worked together
And are too mean to go to the pub

Now Terry, he likes Cappuccino
And Tony can't make up his mind
One week its a tall Americano
And the next week it's Latte, like mine

With rolls filled with Sausage or Bacon
Our breakfast is almost complete
Apart from the moaning and groaning
Which is probably the reason we meet

We talk about all our aches and pains
And stents and Lord only knows what
Then one of us says it's a little bit chilly
And one of us says that he's hot

We talk about health wealth and happiness
And we laugh at each others expense
The Three Musketeers facing life's later years
And trying to make it make sense

We're like an old peoples support group
And we share all our troubles away
But when one of us turns up a little bit late
You can bet that it's his turn to pay

We order another three coffees
Then one of us goes for a leak
We adjourn this meeting of the Old Gits club
And we'll meet again Tuesday next week..

It's Nice to go Travelling ...

Well, here we are back from our holidays
And the suntan's beginning to fade
The Jack Daniels. beer and tequila we drank
Will give way to R Whites Lemonade

The Steak meals and Shrimp Jambalaya
And the Nachos with Mexican dips
Will soon become Sausage and Mash and Baked beans
And on Friday, of course, Fish and Chips

The beaches we left in Miami
And our time on the Florida Keys
The parks and the fun will all roll into one
And soon become Clacton on Sea

My body clock's all up the whassname
I'm living on Florida time
The washing machine's switched to turbo
And my tee shirts are out on the line

But it's good to be back to be honest
And sleeping back in my own bed
It's nice to go travelling but it's nice to come home
As I think Frank Sinatra once said

Umbrella

What's the protocol with an umbrella ?
When you're walking and it's pouring down with rain
If you hit somebody's brolly do you turn and say you're sorry
Or just carry on and do the same again

And when you walk toward a crowd of people
Do you lift your brolly up above their heads
Or do you just make out to try and keep it low to keep you dry
And pretend you didn't hear what someone said

And when you walk into a covered market
Like Spitalfields or even Covent Garden
And forget to put the brolly down
and all around you sneer and frown
Do you care when someone snotty begs your pardon

Or when you go into a shop
and look and think the rain may stop
Do you close your brolly straight away
Or do that close and open thing
and up and down against the spring
And cover everybody with your spray

Do you own the rain on your umbrella
If it drips down someone's neck are you to blame
What's the protocol with an umbrella
When you're walking and it's pouring down with rain

The Golden Fillet

We were down near Clacton in Essex today,
At a place called Holland on sea
We fancied a nice bit of Fish and Chips,
For our lunch, the Mrs and Me

So we popped into the Golden Fillet
On the advice of my Sister in law
We knew that we'd made the correct decision
As soon as we walked through the door

The guy with the beard was a little bit weird
But a pretty girl served us our food
The portions were large but I thought I'd take charge
And at least eat as much as I could

I went for the Rock and Chips myself
A choice I will never regret
The fish was a dish that I just couldn't miss
And the chips were as good as they get

A nice pot of tea for Mary and Me
And her Sister and friend had the same
The jokes from the staff gave us all a good laugh
And I know we'll go in there again

Pyjamas

Now, I thought by the time I reached sixty
I'd have pretty much seen all there was
Silk shirts and Jeans in reds blues and greens
And not much surprised me because ...

...I come from the East End of London
And we shopped down in Petticoat Lane
Where every new fashion, was met with a passion
And we flocked there like moths to a flame

Suits and boots, and coats in the winter
Tee shirts when summer came round
We all did our best to be suitably dressed
From the top of our heads to the ground

But now I see girls in their P.J's
In Tesco's and out in the street
I saw one in Asda in pink fluffy slippers
And a dressing gown that didn't quite meet

Can somebody help me with this one
Or will it just soon go away
Pyjamas are fine in the right place and time
But not in the cold light of day

Now I know that your jammas are comfy
That's why they're nightime attire
You wear them in bed or sometimes instead
When your sitting in front of the fire

But not when you're going out shopping
Or just popping out for a chat
Or I'll go out Monday, in my Winceyette Onesie
And nobody wants to see that.

The Unknown Soldier

It's true, I went away to war and never left that foreign shore
We won, or lost, I'm still not sure
I am the Unknown soldier

I only did what I was told, I wasn't brave, I wasn't bold
And yes, I wanted to grow old,
I am the Unknown Soldier

To fight against men wearing different colours,
In the darkness you couldn't tell us from the others
All missing our girlfriends, our wives and our mothers,
I am the Unknown Soldier

So, wear a Poppy, say a prayer, let me know that you still care
Or tell me, Why did I go there ?
I am the Unknown Soldier

Over the Hill

I wouldn't say I was over the hill
But I'm getting quite close to the top
And I have to say some of this old people stuff
Has caught me a bit on the hop

Like saying the things that my mum used to say
And looking a lot like my dad
And singing along to a Max Bygraves song
While the grandchildren think I've gone mad

Going out in a tee shirt in summer
But taking a jacket in case
Waffling on about when I was young
With a big stupid grin on my face

Going for a walk around Lakeside
And having to stop for a wee
Going into a posh coffee shop
And ordering a nice pot of tea

Buying a packet of Werther's Originals
And keeping them all to myself
Buying a copy of Pie and Mash 2
And keeping it on my book shelf

Going into McDonald's for breakfast
And wanting a knife and fork
Looking bemused and dazed and confused
When I hear how the young people talk

Falling asleep in the armchair
And farting when I get up
I wouldn't say I was over the hill
But I'm getting quite close to the top

Fears, Phobias and Superstitions

Now, I'm not good with wide open spaces
Or for that matter closed in ones either
I'm a bit Agoraphobic and a bit Claustrophobic
And Lifts bring me out in a fever

I'm not great with heights to be honest
And I'm not at my best in a crowd
I'm not keen on needles, bees, snakes or beetles
And spiders should not be allowed

I never eat meat on a Friday
And I try not to walk under ladders
I don't like the dark or big dogs that bark
Or small dogs that yap for that matter

I'm a bit scared of big roller coasters
And Halloween gives me the willies
Does anyone here have these phobias and fears
Or is it just me being silly

No, none of it's true to be honest
Except the lifts, spiders and snakes
But the one I forgot and the worst of the lot
Is that aeroplanes give me the shakes

It's not that I'm frightened of flying
It's crashing I'm worried about
With all these fears, phobias and Superstitions
It's a wonder I ever go out

Easter Eggs

Well, here we are it's Easter time,
And there's chocolate everywhere
I've handed out the Easter Eggs,
But seem to have one spare

I'll just have a roll call of who I gave what to
And soon find out where I went wrong
I know what we got and I know who had what
So let's face it, it shouldn't take long

First of all the Great Grandkids,
Though Connie I thought was too young
But Johnnie and Grayson and Florence,
I made sure that they all got one

Then Sam and Teresa, they both got Malteezers,
Millie and Robyn and John
Jazmin and Chris and Tiernie and Pops
And Maizie and Reg were all done

Mick and Elaine, They both got the same,
Mellissa and Adam and Steph
So while I'm full sure that I bought Twenty four,
Why have I still got one left

There was one for my Brother and one for my Muvver,
And Teresa and Jan have had theirs
And apart from the one with Mary's name on,
There still seems to be one upstairs

And it's Fruit and Nut ... Happy Days ...

First Class

We flew out in Virgin economy
But coming home wasn't the same
For the first time since Brexit, or since records began
I turned left when I got on the plane

I sat in my seat and I put up my feet
Before changing, into my pyjamas
The champagne was cold and you won't need to be told
I was treated like that Judith Chalmers

I had the three courses for dinner
With soup and a nice peppered steak
And a glass of red wine, I was doin just fine
Followed up with the Cherry Cheesecake

My seat transformed into a flat bed
With a pillow and duvet as well
I slipped the condiment set into my bag
I'm not used to all this, you can tell

The girls were so nice and they asked at least twice
If I wanted the Port and the Cheese ...
...with the red onion chutney, well anyone but me
Would have probably answered yes please

But my stomach was now full to bursting
Those airmiles had finally paid off
But next time I might just get on and turn right
I dread to think how much this costs

West Ham Supporter

I've been a West Ham supporter now
For better that fifty odd years
I've cheered from the stands with the rest of the fans
And I've also shed a few tears

I've stood with my mates and watched all the greats,
Like Budgie and Bobby and Bonzo
Trevor and Geoff and even Clyde Best
Dicksie and Robson and Paolo

I've relived the stories of F.A.Cup glories,
Seen Relegation and seen Promotion
We've beat Man United and got all excited
And then lost to in the League Cup to Luton

We've signed some big names
Who have changed a few games
And some of them stayed for the fight
And signed a few wrong 'uns who didn't belong
And just never turned up on the night

Players and mangers come and go,
Fortunes always hiding
Only the badge remains the same
And we don't need reminding

...

We've blown our bubbles down Barking Road
And in the Boleyn Ground
And all around the country
When the Hammers come to town

And now we've moved over to Stratford
And our future's a little uncertain
And our Happy Hammer, smile and a song
Seems to have gone for a burton

It's no good us moaning and wingeing
That only adds to the fears
I've been a West Ham supporter now
For better that fifty odd years

Anyone for Tennis

I've been watching some of the Tennis
From the tournament south of the Thames
I hope that the players ain't parked their cars there
Or they won't see them babies again

I don't know that much about tennis
But the scoring's quite easy to catch
It's fifteen and thirty, forty and duece
Advantage and Game set and Match

Now I don't know the names of the players
And there's others I just can't pronounce
But the way that they swerve while receiving the serve
Like an animal waiting to pounce

Now when it comes to the ladies
I must say they all look the same
But there was two pretty girls with blonde pony tails
And one won it ... Oh what was her name?

I've just seen Pat Cash and John McEnroe
Surley they ain't going to play
I think we might get, to the best of five sets
But it could take the rest of the day

....

...

My money's on whathisname Jokavic
Though Federer's in with a shout
And I do like the way that that Spanish boy plays
I do hope he don't get knocked out

Well anyway, back to Sue Barker
To see who's on court number one
Oh look it's the girl with the blonde pony tail
And she's playing a girl with a bun

Anyone for tennis

Tiffany's gonna be Married

Ryanair have run out Prosecco
On the morning flight going to Spain
The girls who were on the hen party
Said they won't fly with this lot again

Now things are about to get ugly
And the bridesmaids are getting quite loud
One dips in her bag 'cos she fancies a fag
But we all know that that's not allowed

It's a quarter past nine in the morning
And it's too late to stop drinking now
So they're trying the lemonade spritzer
But it's just not the same thing somehow

But I think when they finish the first one
The second one won't taste as bad
And the third will be just what they wanted
Just as we come in too land

But the Bride's mum is getting all weepy
As she knocks back her red wine and coke
And the maid of honour who I think is called Donna
Is snogging with some Spanish bloke

...

...

You see, Tiffany's gonna be married
So she needs to be pissed all weekend
But her whole girly crew will know what to do
To see this don't happen again

I'm sure when they get where they're going
They'll be back on the real stuff again
But Ryanair have run out of Prosecco
On the morning flight going to Spain

I Had the Breakfast Sampler

I had the breakfast sampler from the Ihop
The one they do for over fifty fives
Egg and bacon, ham, hash browns and sausage
And a pancake, what a time to be alive

And then I had a blackened chicken sandwich
With chips of course and sauce you understand
We took it to the beach and with some pineapple and peach
We had a little picnic on the sand

I had a chocolate milkshake from McDonald's
And a cookie, just because they were so cheap
Then we walked back to the shore and thinking I could eat no more
I sat down and just drifted off to sleep

When I woke up I felt a little thirsty
So reached into the cool box for a beer
And after that went down alright, I popped another Miller light
I wasn't driving, let me make that clear

I went down for the Golden Corral buffet
Fifteen bucks a head, all you can eat
There was chicken steak and prawns, mashed potato, chips and corn
Finished with a dish of something sweet

I don't feel very well now ... I think I may have picked up a bug ...   xx

Valentines Day

Tomorrow is gonna be Valentines Day
Though I haven't got anything planned
Perhaps I should do her, Breakfast in Bed
Or slip something Gold in her hand

I know, I'll buy her some Roses
All sprinkled with fresh drops of rain
When she opens her eyes she'll get a surprise
She'll think I've forgotten ... again

Or maybe a big box of chocolates
In a box that's shaped like a heart
And a big card that says, I'll Love you always
At least that would be a good start

Perhaps a trip out to a restaurant
For a romantic dinner for two
Now I will have to book so I'll have a good look
Cos I just don't think Nando's will do

So I'll spend today planning tomorrow
And do all things that I've said
The day for all Lovers, the young and the others
Valentines ... The fourteenth of Feb ....

Oh bugger ... That's today ain't it ? ...

oops! ...xx

My Cockney Accent

My Cockney accent drops in and out
That's just the way that it is
It's not that I'm using my telephone voice
The fact is it's always like this

Sometimes it's stronger than others
And no, I'm not putting it on
I open my mouth and the words just come out
You should hear me when I sing a song

Sometimes I sing like Sinatra
And sometimes like old Willie Nelson
I once tried to sing like that Whitney Houston
But I found out that weren't gonna happen

Sometimes I talk like Alf Garnett
And at others I sound more refined
And when I'm recording my poems
I never know which voice I'll find

I laugh when I'm told I'm not Cockney
By someone who ain't got a clue
I come from Mile End where the people all blend
And that's why we talk like we do

So Lionel Bart, Delboy or Albert
Or even Frank Butcher sometimes
It don't really matter, it's just some old chatter
But believe me it's really all mine

After the Storm

I'd first like thank you for coming
It's lovely to see you all here
It's a shame that it isn't the weekend
I'd have put out some nuts and some beer

But as today is a school-day
And for that matter, tomorrow is too
I've just done some tea and a biscuit
So, I'm afraid that you'll have to make do

So sit down and make yourself comfy
If you have five minutes to spare
We'll just have a chat about this and of that
And let the time pass without care

Did you see the football on telly last night?
A good result I would have thought
And as for that storm, well that wasn't the norm
And look at the havoc it brought

Well, when I say havoc, it brought down my fence
To be honest, it blew out one panel
And somebody's washing wound up in my garden
Two towels and a dark blue face flannel

Well, that's enough excitement for one morning
So drink your tea and then get on your way
I've got a lot of things to do, I can't just sit and chat with you
I've got to fix that garden fence today ... xx

A Smile and a Song

I woke up this morning with a smile and a song
It was then that I realised that something was wrong
Who was that singing at this time of day
And what was I smiling about anyway

Well the singing was the radio alarm clock
And Mary had got in the shower
She usually makes sure the thing is turned off
So I'm not woken up at this hour

She'd obviously gotten up early
And hit the wrong button it seems
With nothing to lose she probably hit snooze
Without waking me from my dreams

Well the song that was on was Rod Stewart
Singing "You wear it well"
A favourite of mine from a long ago time
So I joined in the chorus as well

And then they played one by The Beatles
"I saw her standing there"
Well when I say standing, she passed by on the landing
To the spare room, towel drying her hair

But I still hadn't worked out the smiling
Then it dawned on me out of the blue
It's Monday and you lot are going to work
And I'm retired with nothing to do ...xx

All you Need is Love

My buns of steel are tubs of lard
And my six pack's a party seven
I used to go out and party hard
But now I'm in bed by eleven

My long wavy hair with plenty to spare
That once was my crowning glory
Is now something I lack, except down my back
But then that's a whole different story

I can't see a thing without glasses
And I can't hear as well as I could
I creak when I walk and croak when I talk
And carry more weight than I should

My memory is sometimes a problem
And my joints aren't as supple and strong
My skin isn't quite so elastic
But most bits are still where they belong

But I still have my friends and family
And we fit like a hand in a glove
I think that you might, find the Beatles were right
When they told us that All you need is Love

As I Wander

As I wander, far and wide, this Green and Pleasant Land
From farm lands hills and forests to the soft and golden sand
The highlands to the lowlands where forever cattle grazed
Through all the compass points I never cease to be amazed

The diversity of plant life and the colours nature shows
Through blazing summer sunshine to the bitter winter snows
Our cities and our countryside, our seasides and our towns
All full of the familiar and the welcome sights and sounds

Church bells ring and Blackbirds sing and all in easy reach
Male voice choirs, dreamy spires and donkeys on the beach
Village Greens and Cricket on a Sunday afternoon
Brass Bands play in banstands, and the Summer ends too soon

Proud of where we come from, proud of where we live
England, Ireland, Scotland, Wales, these islands give and give
The ancient and the modern stand together hand in glove
Give thanks and praise this Green and Pleasant Land
that we so love

Blueberry and Lemon Cake

I made a Blueberry and Lemon cake
I've never made this one before
I followed the recipe from the United States
But I must say I wasn't too sure

I've never used cups as a measurement
Only for drinking my tea
I bought some new scales in the Asda Spring sales
And now find they're no good to me

So with two cups of flour and one cup of sugar
And of course a nice cup of Typhoo
A half cup of oil, some lemon and salt
Some vanilla and sour cream too

Two Eggs and some Baking Powder
And cooked for an hour 'til it's done
And a bottle of cold Crabbie's real Ginger Beer
While I'm watching A Place in the Sun

Well once it was out of the oven
I must say it looked good to me
I had a big slice and it wasn't half nice
Washed down with a nice cup of tea ...

Still on the Green Side of the Grass

Now, as I'm getting older
And more things begin to ache
I sit and watch the telly
And find it hard to stay awake

I've got seventeen pairs of reading glasses
From plus 1 to 2.5
And a pair of prescription sunglasses
That I have to wear when I drive

I've given up the cigarettes
And don't drink very much
I'm a fan of the Antiques Roadshow
And crumbly chocolate fudge

I tend to fart when I laugh too hard
Or when I stand up or sit down
I got a new pair of slippers for Christmas
And a towelling dressing gown

Whenever I go for a blood test,
I end up getting a bruise
And I have to sit down for a breather
After I've done up my shoes

I often go upstairs and then
Can't remember quite what for
But I may as well go in and use the loo,
As I'm passing the door

...

...

My hip hurts when it's raining
And so does my left knee
And sometimes the flippin' indigestion
Gets the better of me
But at least I've still got all my own teeth
And enjoy a nice bit of toffee
I don't take drugs, except in mugs
And it's caffeine that's found in my coffee

But life is what you make it
And this life's been good to me
And I'm still enjoying every day
To a greater or lesser degree

To quote the late George Harrison
Who said All things must pass
I'm older it's true but just like you
I'm still on the Green side of the grass

Thank You ...xx

I never know what's coming next,
I never know what to expect
I write a word, a line of text
And there it is a poem

I start out with something to say
Then turn it 'round another way
Some words go and some words stay
And somehow it keeps growing

It seems to work out in the end
Some are witty, some pretend
Some will drive you round the bend
Without me even knowing

Some are poignant, some are true
Some might mean something to you
The odd line borrowed, the odd line blue
The Cockney in me showing

It's nothing though unless it's read
The written word becomes the said
That's not me, that's you instead
You keep the juices flowing

Thank You ...xx

Lightning Source UK Ltd.
Milton Keynes UK
UKHW021105081118
331988UK00005B/593/P